Popular Mechanics

Band Saw Fundamentals

Rick Peters

Hearst Books

A Division of Sterling Publishing Co., Inc.

New York

Production Staff

Design: Triad Design Group

Cover Design: Celia Fuller

Photography: Christopher J. Vendetta

Contributing Writer: Cheryl A. Romano

Cover Photo: Christopher J. Vendetta

Illustrations: Triad Design Group

Copy Editor: Barbara McIntosh Webb

Page Layout: Triad Design Group

Index: Nan Badgett

Every effort has been made to ensure that all information in this book is accurate. However, due to differing conditions, tools, and individual skills, the publisher cannot be responsible for injuries, losses, or other damages which may result from the use of information in this book.

Note: The safety guards were removed for clarity in many of the photographs in this book. Make sure to always use all safety devices according to the manufacturers' instructions.

Library of Congress Cataloging-in-Publication Data Available.

10 9 8 7 6 5 4 3 2 1

Published by Hearst Books
A Division of Sterling Publishing Co., Inc.
387 Park Avenue South, New York, NY 10016

Popular Mechanics and Hearst Books are registered trademarks of Hearst Communications, Inc.

www.popularmechanics.com

Distributed in Canada by Sterling Publishing
c/o Canadian Manda Group, 165 Dufferin Street
Toronto, Ontario, Canada M6K 3H6

Distributed in Australia by Capricorn Link (Australia) Pty. Ltd.
P.O. Box 704, Windsor, NSW 2756 Australia

For information about custom editions, special sales, premium and corporate purchases, please contact Sterling Special Sales Department at 800-805-5489 or specialsales@sterlingpub.com.

Manufactured in China

Sterling ISBN 13: 978-1-58816-522-0
ISBN 10: 1-58816-522-1

Contents

ACKNOWLEDGMENTS

For all their help, advice, and support, I offer special thanks to:

Sara Ruth from Delta Machinery, for providing two hardworking Delta band saws, well-made band saw blades and their capability-expanding height attachment kit, Porter-Cable's portable band saw, and technical assistance.

Abigail Bradford with Hitachi Tools, for supplying their well-made band saw and technical information.

Amy Montgomery with Ryobi Technologies, Inc., for providing their well-thought-out band saw and technical assistance.

Chris Daley with DeWalt Tools, for supplying their tough portable band saw and technical information.

Catherine Helshoj with Laguna Tools, for the firm's impressive band saws and accessories, including their ceramic guide system and impressive Resaw King blades, and technical assistance.

Brent Gantenbein with Kreg Tool Company, for supplying premier band saw accessories, including their well-designed precision band saw fence.

Lee Perez with Carter Products Company, Inc., for supplying their smooth-running ball-bearing guide system and other band saw accessories.

Christopher Vendetta, for taking photographs under less-than-desirable conditions.

Rob Lembo and the crew at Triad Design Group, for superb illustrations and layout skills, whose talents are evident on every page of this book.

Barb Webb, copyediting whiz, for ferreting out mistakes and gently suggesting corrections.

Heartfelt thanks to my constant inspiration: Cheryl, Lynne, Will, and Beth.

INTRODUCTION

When most woodworkers think of a band saw, they envision a machine that cuts intricate curves even in thick stock. And that's true—a band saw is more than capable of handling this task like no other power tool can. But a band saw is capable of doing a lot more than cutting curves. For starters, a properly tuned band saw can rip, crosscut, miter, and bevel. It's a great joint-making machine as well. Did you know that you can easily and precisely cut lap joints and tenons on the band saw? A band saw can also be used to cut faux mortises and even dovetails. What's more, the band saw can handle another job better than any other tool—resawing thick stock into thin boards. You can make your own lumber with a band saw—custom-cut to any thickness. You can even slice your own solid veneer.

The band saw is such a versatile machine that many woodworkers—including many famous ones—believe the band saw should be a novice woodworker's first major tool purchase. This is particularly true for those woodworkers for whom shop space is at a premium. No other tool packs such varied capabilities in such a small package as the band saw.

In this book, we'll help you choose and accessorize a band saw. We'll take you through all of the basic techniques like ripping, crosscutting, and cutting curves. Then we cover advanced techniques like making compound cuts (always wanted to make cabriole legs?) and how to resaw and cut a variety of woodworking joints. We've included detailed plans for a dozen jigs and fixtures you can build to expand the capabilities of your saw. Maintenance and repair is laid out in detail so you can keep your band saw running in tip-top shape. And the final chapter details projects you can build using just the band saw or using the band saw as the primary tool.

Armed with this information, we hope you'll spend some quality time with a band saw to discover just what one of these amazing machines is capable of.

—James Meigs

Editor-in-Chief, *Popular Mechanics*

1 Choosing a Band Saw

Of all the stationary power tools out there for working wood, the band saw is the most versatile. Quite a statement, but it's true if you think about it. You can crosscut and rip on a band saw as you would with a table saw or miter saw. You can create myriad woodworking joints with a band saw, including dovetails (try that on a table saw). And unlike on a table saw or miter saw, you can cut intricate curves. Add to this the increased thickness capacity of even the smallest bench-top band saws, and you have a machine that's capable of handling a tremendous variety of woodworking tasks.

As a matter of fact, many woodworkers feel that the band saw is the most important tool in the shop— some don't even have a table saw. Woodworking greats like James Krenov and Sam Maloof use band saws extensively to craft their exquisite furniture. In this chapter, we'll show you what to look for—and what to look out for—when shopping for a band saw of your own.

Band saws come in all shapes and sizes, from diminutive portable band saws to large heavy-duty versions. All these saws use a continuous blade or band to plow through wood, including straight, angled, and curved cuts.

Bench-Top Band Saws

Regardless of their size, all band saws are very similar and operate much the same way. A continuous blade or "band" is stretched between two wheels: One is driven by a motor or pulley and is fixed in place; the other adjusts up and down to apply tension and tilts to "track" or keep the blade centered on the wheels. A slotted table fits around the blade to provide a work surface for cutting. The table usually tilts to allow for angled cuts. Added features may include a rip fence and a miter gauge.

Bench-top band saws are designed to rest on a workbench (although most now come with their own stand) and often employ a small direct-drive motor (typically $1/2$ horsepower). That is, the motor shaft turns the drive wheel of the saw directly. (For more on motors and drive types, see page 15.) A bench-top band saw is a good choice for a woodworker with limited shop space. Its diminutive size and light weight make it easy to store the saw out of the way when not in use.

Bench-top band saws typically have smaller throats and cutting capacities than stationary or floor-model band saws (for more on cutting capacities, see page 12). These smaller saws can handle many cutting tasks but should be used sparingly for heavy work such as resawing, as they're just not built for this type of work. Resawing (cutting a board through its thickness) requires a wide blade, a stout motor, and a lot of tension on the blade. Most bench-top band saws can only take up to a $1/2$"-wide blade ($3/4$" and wider is recommended for resawing), have a small motor ($1/2$ hp), and employ a frame that can't handle the pressure of a highly tensioned blade. For this type of work, you're better off with a floor-model band saw (see the opposite page).

ANATOMY OF A PORTABLE BAND SAW

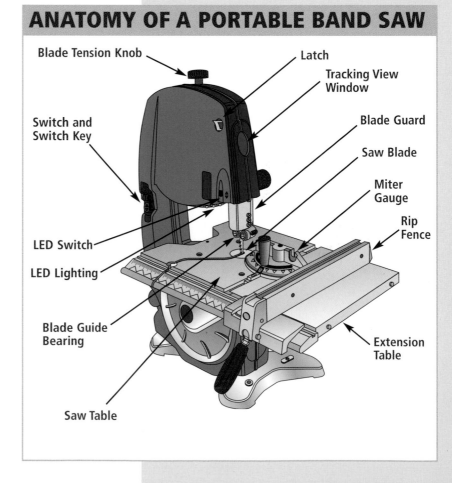

Blade Tension Knob

Latch

Tracking View Window

Switch and Switch Key

Blade Guard

Saw Blade

Miter Gauge

Rip Fence

LED Switch

LED Lighting

Blade Guide Bearing

Extension Table

Saw Table

ANATOMY OF A FLOOR-MODEL BAND SAW

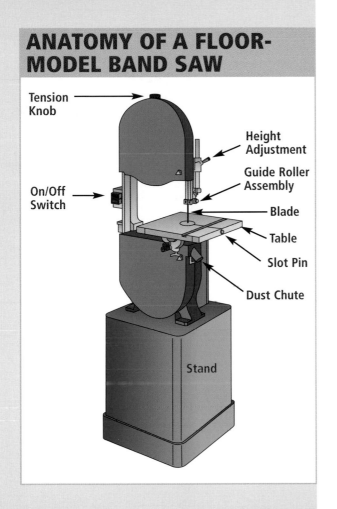

Tension Knob

Height Adjustment

Guide Roller Assembly

On/Off Switch

Blade

Table

Slot Pin

Dust Chute

Stand

Floor-Model Band Saws

A floor model or stationary band saw is a larger version of the bench-top saw. It's built with heavy castings and has larger capacities. The size that's most often found in the woodworking shop is a 14" saw that can handle stock up to 6" in thickness. The 14" refers to the throat depth—the distance from the blade to the frame—and identifies the maximum width you can cut. For example, a 14" saw can cut to the center of a 28"-wide board.

Heavier castings may seem insignificant, but the stout frame of a floor-model band saw is what allows it to handle tough jobs like resawing. You can crank up the tension on a heavy-duty frame without worry. Additionally, most floor-model band saws accept blades as large as 3/4" to 1" in width. And most come with a 3/4- to 1½-hp motor. Combine these features and you have a saw that can cut a 6"-wide board in half along its thickness.

BASE TYPES
Floor-model or stationary band saws are available with either open or closed bases.

Open base. Most band saws come with an open base. On the plus side, plenty of air can circulate around the motor to keep it cool. The downside is that this air is often dust-laden and can work its way into the motor, shortening its life.

Closed base. A closed base costs more but makes it easier to collect and convey dust and chips to a collector. It also protects the motor from dust. A well-designed closed base will have side louvers for ventilation that can be covered with inexpensive filter material to keep out harmful dust.

Industrial Band Saws

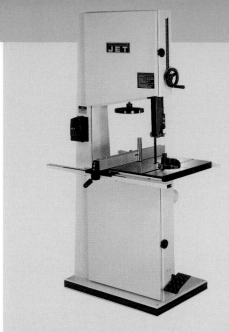

Heavy-duty or industrial band saws are basically floor-model band saws on steroids. These massive machines often tip the scales at over 500 pounds. They feature huge cutting capacities, powerful motors, and the best castings and parts money can buy. Although found more frequently in professional cabinet shops and in manufacturing, some woodworkers need the extra capacity these saws offer.

Motor power ranges from 2 to a whopping 6.6 horsepower. Throat capacity (maximum cut width) ranges from 15" to 24" (imagine cutting a sheet of plywood in half on a band saw). Maximum depth of cut varies from 12" to 20". Although the idea of cutting something that's 20" thick might seem unbelievable, woodturners who specialize in turning large bowls frequently need to make cuts this thick.

The wheels on these saws are typically so large that there is no stand or base. The saw frame itself is the base and rests on the floor. In addition to weighing a lot, these saws also cost a lot. If your budget can afford one of these saws—and if it will fit in your shop—an industrial band saw is a joy to use, as it can cut through almost anything like a hot knife through butter.

INDUSTRIAL BAND SAW ANATOMY

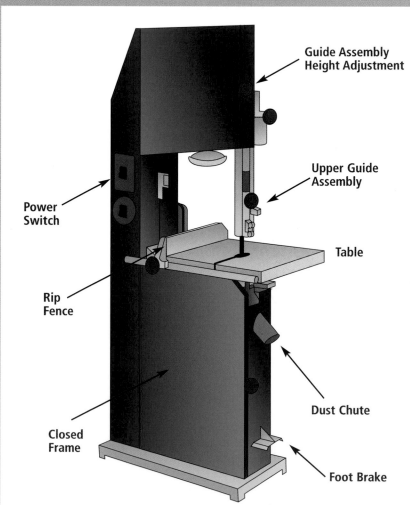

Guide Assembly Height Adjustment

Upper Guide Assembly

Power Switch

Table

Rip Fence

Dust Chute

Closed Frame

Foot Brake

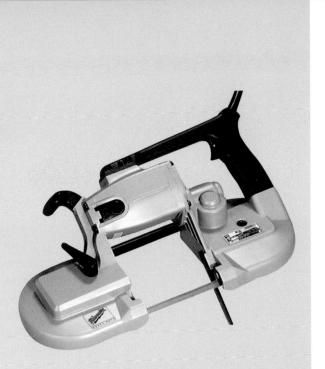

Portable Band Saws

Although designed primarily for cutting metal, a portable band saw can also cut wood. The big difference between a portable band saw and a stationary saws is with a portable band saw you take the saw to the work instead of the other way around. Portable band saws are most often used horizontally to cut so that gravity works for you instead of against you (for more on using a portable band saw, see page 80).

Some portable band saw manufacturers offer stands and/or clamp attachments that connect to or hold the saw so you can make cuts easier. A clamp attachment fits onto the saw and is designed to hold a workpiece securely in a vise. A pivot on the attachment allows you to pivot the saw uniformly into the workpiece for an accurate cut. A stand holds the saw vertically like a regular band saw and has a table that's used as a work surface for cutting.

Virtually all portable band saws use 44$^7/_8$"-long blades and have similar cutting capacities—typically 4$^1/_2$" by 4$^1/_2$". They excel at cutting metal, and you'd be surprised how easily they'll cut though steel pipe, bars, and rebar. If you've ever spent time with a hacksaw trying to cut a piece of stout metal, you'll appreciate the speed and effortlessness that a portable band saw can offer.

ANATOMY OF A PORTABLE BAND SAW

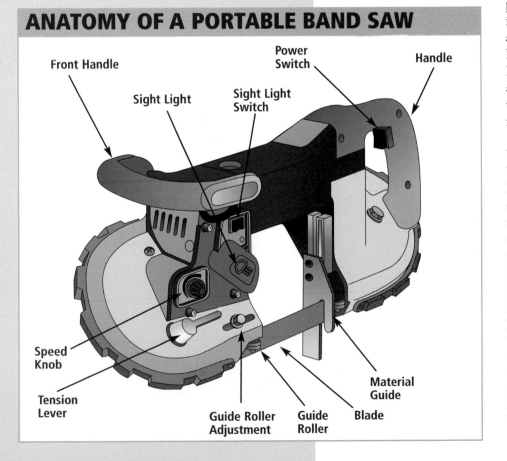

Front Handle

Sight Light

Power Switch

Sight Light Switch

Handle

Speed Knob

Tension Lever

Guide Roller Adjustment

Guide Roller

Blade

Material Guide

Saw Capacity

Band saws are typically classified by their cutting capacity—in particular, the throat capacity or maximum width of cut and the maximum depth of cut, as illustrated in the top drawing. Additionally, table size is often called out in specifications (as illustrated in the top drawing), but it has little to do with the cutting capacity of the saw.

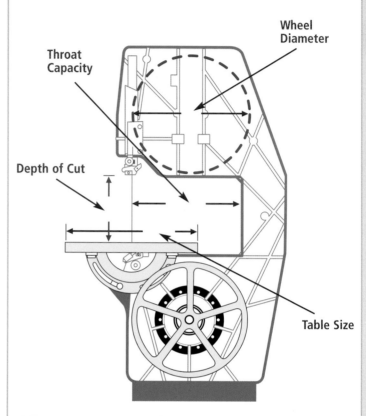

Throat capacity

Throat capacity is the distance from the blade to the frame of the saw. This defines the widest piece you can cut. Some manufacturers double this and say that you can cut to the center of a panel twice that width. For example, if the throat capacity is 12", they'll say you can cut to the center of a 24"-wide panel. Obviously, the larger the throat capacity, the better. Throat capacity is the most common classification for a band saw. For example, the throat capacity on the Ryobi saw shown in the middle photo is 10"—so the saw is referred to as a 10" band saw.

Depth of cut

The maximum depth of cut is the distance from the table surface to the bottom of the upper guide assembly and defines the maximum thickness of stock you can cut. (The depth of cut on the Hitachi band saw shown in the bottom photo is 5".) Although we've always found 6" to be sufficient, some manufacturers sell an optional riser or height attachment that extends the upper wheel to increase the maximum depth of cut, as described on the opposite page.

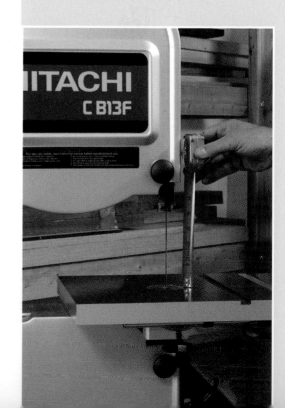

TABLE TYPES

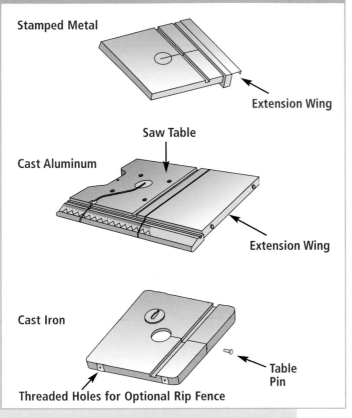

Stamped Metal

Extension Wing

Saw Table

Cast Aluminum

Extension Wing

Cast Iron

Table Pin

Threaded Holes for Optional Rip Fence

Table types

Although it doesn't affect the cutting capacities of a band saw, the type and size of the table can impact its usefulness. A small table provides too small a work surface to fully support a workpiece during a cut. The three most common types of table you'll find are stamped metal, cast aluminum, and cast iron, as illustrated in the top drawing. There are pros and cons of each type. Stamped metal keeps costs down, but tends to warp. Its light weight also does nothing to suppress vibration. Cast aluminum is inexpensive and also light and so doesn't help with vibration. But you'll never have to worry about the surface rusting, as is so common with cast-iron tables. Cast-iron tables are machined flat and true, and their weight helps dampen vibration. The only disadvantage of a cast-iron table is that it's prone to rust—but this is easily handled with a little preventive maintenance, as described on pages 140–142.

HEIGHT ATTACHMENTS

A height attachment increases the cutting capacity of your saw, as shown in the photos at right. Although kits vary from one manufacturer to another, most contain a riser block that fits between the upper and lower halves of the band saw frame, a longer post for the blade guard, and a blade guard extension, as shown in the left photo. These kits are fairly straightforward to install; see pages 150–153 for more on installing a height attachment.

Before. The cutting capacity of a standard 14" Delta band saw as shown here is 6¼" using a 93½" blade.

After. With the addition of Delta's height attachment, the saw's cutting capacity is increased to 12¼" using a 105" blade.

Wheel Configuration

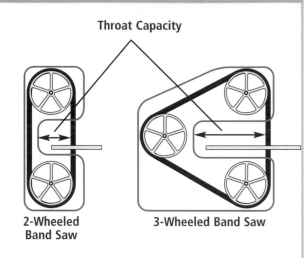

Throat Capacity

2-Wheeled Band Saw

3-Wheeled Band Saw

Most band saws employ two wheels to rotate the blade; some band saws use three, as illustrated in the top drawing. The advantage of using three wheels is it increases the throat capacity or maximum width of cut. The disadvantage of this setup is it can be a lot more difficult to keep a blade tracking properly on three wheels. All three of the wheels must be in the same plane, as described on page 132. Three-wheeled saws were much more common in the past. They have become mostly outdated with the increased-capacity industrial-sized saws as described on page 10.

Typical wheel sizes

On two-wheeled band saws, the diameter of the saw's wheels is roughly the same as the throat size; that is, a 14" band saw will typically use 14"-diameter wheels. In most cases, the throat capacity is typically $1/4$" or so less than the wheel diameter because of the blade guard next to the column frame of the saw. For example, a 14" Delta band saw has an actual throat size of $13^3/4$". But it's a generally accepted practice to round this up to 14". Typical wheel sizes for portable, bench-top, floor-model, and industrial band saws are illustrated in the bottom drawing.

COMMON WHEEL DIAMETERS

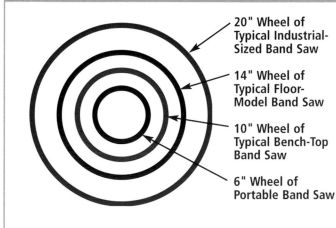

20" Wheel of Typical Industrial-Sized Band Saw

14" Wheel of Typical Floor-Model Band Saw

10" Wheel of Typical Bench-Top Band Saw

6" Wheel of Portable Band Saw

WHEEL MATERIALS

There are two common materials used to make band saw wheels: cast aluminum and cast iron.

Cast iron. The heavy cast-iron wheels on the Wilke band saw shown here help reduce vibration. If you're looking to buy a band saw with cast-iron wheels, make sure the wheels are precision-balanced. Otherwise you can end up with more, rather than less, vibration.

Cast aluminum. The lightweight but sturdy multi-spoke wheel on the Delta band saw shown here is a typical cast-aluminum wheel. The wheel is covered with a rubber band to protect the blade.

Motor Drive and Power

Much of how well a band saw will perform will depend on its motor and how it drives the wheels. The two most common drive types are direct-drive and belt-drive.

Direct-drive

Direct-drive motors are typically found only on portable and bench-top band saws. These motors tend to be small—around 1/2 horsepower. The drive shaft of the motor connects directly to the lower or drive wheel of the band saw as shown in the left photo. The advantage to this is that power is transferred directly and there's little chance of vibration from misaligned belts or pulleys. Unless the motor has a variable-speed control, you can't change speeds like you can with a belt-driven saw.

Belt-drive

Most floor and industrial band saws use a belt-and-pulley system to transfer power from the motor to the drive wheel, as shown in the top right photo. Although this can add vibration (due to misaligned pulleys or a worn belt), it does allow you to change speeds by using step pulleys. Some saw makers offer speed kits for their saws, as described in the sidebar

below. Belt-drive systems are also easier on the saw, as the belt will flex on startup and dampen some of the torque that would be passed on directly to the drive wheel and blade. The buffer provided by the belt helps reduce blade breakage and wear and tear on bearings.

Motor power

Motor power is generally listed in horsepower. When used to describe a tool, horsepower is an indication of how capable the tool is of performing its tasks. The rated horsepower of a tool is the torque level at which the motor can be run continuously without exceeding the temperature at which the insulation breaks down. No motor produces usable horsepower unless it is slowed down by applying a mechanical load. With a universal motor, the horsepower is often labeled as "developed" horsepower. Developed horsepower may be 2 to 5 times the continuous-duty rating of a motor. The term "develops 3 hp" is meaningless marketing hype—use the amperage rating instead; as a rule of thumb, the higher the amperage, the more powerful the motor. (Amperage ratings can be found on the motor label as shown in the middle right photo.)

SPEED KITS

Many band saw manufacturers offer speed kits to convert a single-speed saw into a multi-speed saw. These kits commonly consist of a pair of stepped pulleys, and may include an intermediate pulley like the Jet speed kit shown here. It allows any of their 14" band saws to run at three speeds: 735, 1470, and 2350 rpm.

Ergonomics

Almost as important as the capacities and power of a band saw is its ergonomics—that is, how easy and comfortable it is to use the saw. Because there are a number of moving parts that need to be adjusted often on a band saw, it's important to check these out on any saw that you're interested in. The only way to get a feel for a saw's ergonomics is to get your hands on the saw—literally. Visit a home center, check out your friend's saw, or take a day trip to a woodworking show—it'll be time well spent. Operate the upper guide assembly, try out the rip fence and miter gauge, and look particularly closely at how easy or difficult it is to change a blade and make all of the associated adjustments. Changing a blade on a band saw is much more time-consuming than, say, changing the blade on a table saw. So it's important that this be as simple as possible.

Power switches

A power switch on a quality band saw will be easy to operate, be within quick reach, and hold up well over time, like the one shown in the top left photo. The large push buttons of this switch are easy to operate and "toggle" positively when engaged. If children will ever be in your shop, look for a power switch that locks or offers a "key" like the one shown in the Hitachi band saw in the top right photo.

Rip fence

In our opinion, a rip fence is an essential accessory for the band saw. On some saws, this add-on comes standard as shown on the Ryobi saw in the middle photo. If your saw doesn't have a rip fence, you can purchase one from the manufacturer (if offered), buy an after-market fence (see page 33), or make your own (see pages 103–107). Look for a fence that offers built-in stops and can be adjusted to compensate for blade drift (see page 51). If your band saw doesn't have holes in the front of the saw table to accept a fence rail (like the Hitachi shown in the bottom photo), you can build the table and fence as described on pages 99–107.

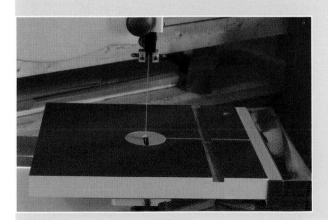

GUIDE ASSEMBLIES

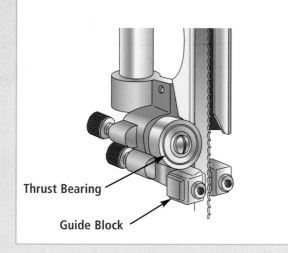

Thrust Bearing

Guide Block

Guide assemblies

In a perfect world, a band saw blade would run straight and true on the wheels without any kind of assistance. Technically, this is true for most saws, as long as you don't make any cuts on the saw. But as soon as you cut into a workpiece, the workpiece exerts pressure on the blade from the front and often from the side. This pressure is sufficient in most cases to knock the blade right off the wheels. To prevent this, all band saw manufacturers add upper and lower guide assemblies to their saws.

Each guide assembly consists of a pair of guide blocks, as illustrated in the top drawing, that sand-

wich the blade from side to side and keep it from deflecting under cutting pressure. There's also a thrust bearing located behind the blade to prevent it from deflecting backwards (more on this below). The upper guide assembly is adjustable up and down to keep the assembly (and guard) as close to the workpiece as possible to offer maximum support; the lower guide assembly is fixed. The guide blocks and thrust bearing on both assemblies are adjustable to handle a variety of blade types and widths.

Ease of adjustment

Virtually every time you replace a blade, you'll need to adjust the guide assemblies. So it's important to find a saw that has stout guide assemblies that are easy to adjust. Look for square guide blocks or roller bearings (near right photo), not round guide blocks like those shown in the far right photo. Round blocks do not fully support the blade as well as square ones. Also, look for adjustments that can be made without tools. Guide assemblies that offer thumbscrew locks and easy-to-adjust knobs make adjusting guide assemblies less of a chore.

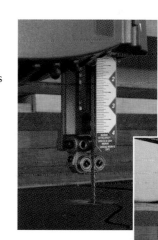

Thrust bearings

You'll find thrust bearings in one of two common configurations: edge- or face-mounted, as illustrated in the bottom drawing. On an edge-mounted bearing, the blade rubs on the edge of the bearing. With a face-mounted bearing, the blade rubs on the bearing's face. Face-mounted thrust bearings are more common, as they offer a larger surface area and tend to wear slower. On an edge-mounted bearing, it's possible to wear a groove in the bearing's edge, which can result in premature bearing failure.

THRUST BEARING OPTIONS

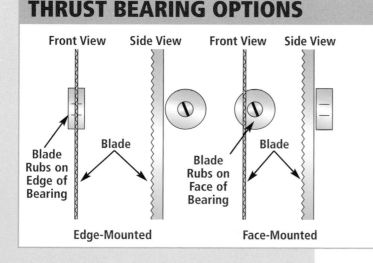

Front View Side View Front View Side View

Blade Rubs on Edge of Bearing

Blade

Blade Rubs on Face of Bearing

Blade

Edge-Mounted

Face-Mounted

Height adjustment

The most frequently adjusted part of a band saw is the upper guide assembly. You adjust its height to match the thickness of the workpiece. It just makes sense, then, that the easier it is to raise and lower the assembly, the better. On some saws, like the Ryobi shown in the top left photo, the height of the assembly is raised and lowered via a rack-and-pinion system. The advantage here is that this allows for easy one-handed adjustment. On many other saws, the guide assembly is simply a post that's locked in place with a knob. To adjust this type of guide assembly, you need to support the assembly with one hand and lock it in place with the other, as shown in the top right photo.

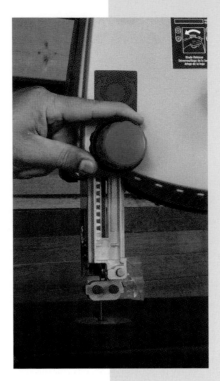

NIFTY FEATURES

Sometimes it's the little details that can make your purchasing decision swing in one direction or the other. All of the features below indicate that some extra thought was put into the design of a band saw.

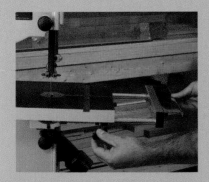

Wing extension. The Hitachi saw shown here comes with a built-in wing extension that serves double duty. First, it offers additional side support for wide workpieces. Second, the wing itself can be raised to serve as a rip fence.

Wheel brushes. Band saws create a lot of dust. Dust can build up on the wheels and cause tracking problems and excess blade and wheel band wear. Delta knows this and added built-in wheel brushes on their 10" ShopMaster band saw, shown here.

Miter gauge storage. Sure it's a little thing, but adding a built-in bracket (as on the Hitachi saw shown here) for storing your miter gauge means you'll never have to search for it again.

The upper wheel on a band saw is adjustable in two directions, up and down, to control tension, and it can be tilted forward and backward to adjust how the blade runs or "tracks" on the wheels. Both of these adjustments are made every time a blade is changed, so it's important that they lock in place positively and are easy to adjust.

Tracking adjustments

The tracking adjustment on the Delta saw shown in the top left photo has a convenient thumbscrew lock. This makes it easy to first loosen the tracking, make the adjustment, and then lock it back in place. On some saws, like the one shown in the top right photo, a wrench is required to loosen the locking mechanism. If possible, consider replacing the nut with an easy-to-use wing nut.

Blade-tension adjustments

On virtually all band saws, blade tension is applied by turning a knob on top of the saw (as shown in the far left photo). This controls the tension on a spring located within the upper housing. This works fine, but it can be tedious if you change blades frequently. Delta recently unveiled a nifty quick-release feature for some of their larger saws, as shown in the bottom photo . In the up position, tension is applied. Pulling the lever down releases tension so you can change blades. The nice thing is if you're putting on the same-width blade, you just raise the lever and the correct amount of tension is instantly applied. Not really earth-shattering, but after we changed a couple of blades on the 14" Delta saw shown here, we got real used to this feature and wished other saws had it as well.

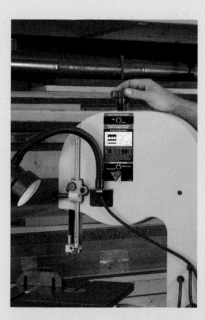

Changing blades

Okay, so you've identified how easy or hard it might be to adjust the guide assemblies, tracking, and tension. How about actually removing the blade? Remember, the saw table is slotted for blade removal. So you still need to determine how much of a challenge it is to get the blade off and out of the saw. Here again, it's the details that matter. Little things like slot location can hinder or help blade removal, as illustrated in the drawing below. Slots that are perpendicular to the front edge of the saw table allow you to virtually pull the blade off the

wheels and straight out. When the slot is parallel to the front edge of the saw table, you'll have to rotate the blade 90 degrees before it can be removed.

Since a slot in the table could cause the table to twist or warp, all band saw makers use some form of keeper to keep the halves of the table aligned. Most common is a pin in the edge of the table that typically needs a wrench to remove it (middle left photo). Some saws (like the Delta ShopMaster shown in the top left photo) use a bolt and wing nut that don't require tools for removal.

Table tilt

The table on a band saw should be able to tilt for angled cuts. Take the time to tilt the table to see how easily it tilts, paying attention to the locking knob and indicator. On most saws, the table bottom fits in half-circle-shaped arms that support the table and allow it tilt as shown in the bottom right photo. Much like the upper guide assembly, adjusting a table like this requires both hands: one to angle the table, and the other to lock it in place. Other saws (like the Delta saw in the middle right photo) employ a rack-and-pinion system that allows one-handed adjustments.

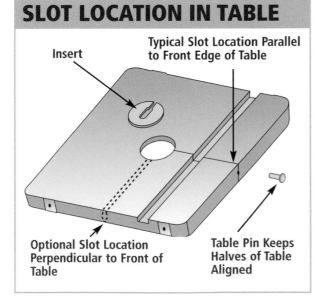

SLOT LOCATION IN TABLE

Insert

Typical Slot Location Parallel to Front Edge of Table

Optional Slot Location Perpendicular to Front of Table

Table Pin Keeps Halves of Table Aligned

◼ RECOMMENDATIONS

Portable Band Saws

Since most portable band saws use the same-length blade and have similar cutting capacities, choosing one really boils down to two things: reputation and price. Go with a name you trust and shop for the best price. Website search engines like Bizrate (www.bizrate.com) make this easy to do. Things to look for when shopping for a portable band saw: variable speeds, a rugged carrying case, spare blades, and a decent warranty. It's also a good idea to check to see where the closest authorized service center is, in case you need parts or repair service. Most manufacturers list locations on their website.

PORTABLE BAND SAWS

Brand/Model	Motor	Ft./Min.	Speed	Max. Cut	Blade Length	Weight (lbs.)
Dewalt 2877	6-amp	82–280	variable	$4\frac{3}{4}" \times 4\frac{3}{4}"$	$44\frac{7}{8}"$	15.5
Grizzly G8692	1-hp	190–262	two	$4\frac{3}{4}" \times 4\frac{3}{4}"$	$44\frac{7}{8}"$	38
Makita 2106	4.5-amp/6.5-amp	200–260	two	$4\frac{1}{2}" \times 4\frac{1}{2}"$	$44\frac{7}{8}"$	25
Milwaukee 6238	4.5-amp/6.5-amp	250–350	two	$4\frac{3}{4}" \times 4\frac{3}{4}"$	$44\frac{7}{8}"$	31
Milwaukee 6232	6-amp	0–350	variable	$4\frac{3}{4}" \times 4\frac{3}{4}"$	$44\frac{7}{8}"$	31
Porter-Cable 9725	4.5-amp/6.5-amp	195–245	two	$3\frac{3}{8}" \times 4\frac{1}{8}"$	$44\frac{7}{8}"$	19
Porter-Cable 7724	6-amp	100–265	variable	$4\frac{1}{2}" \times 4\frac{3}{4}"$	$44\frac{7}{8}"$	18

Bench-Top Band Saws

If shop space and budget are limited, a bench-top band saw is a good choice. Look for a model with at least a $\frac{1}{2}$-hp motor that can handle a wide variety of blade widths, preferably $\frac{1}{8}"$ to $\frac{1}{2}"$. Check to make sure that the stand is sturdy and that the saw comes with all the features you want. Little details like built-in dust collection, standard rip fence and miter gauge, and built-in lights are all worth looking for. As with any band saw, make sure that blade changing is easy and that all the controls are easy to use and comfortable.

BENCH-TOP BAND SAWS

Brand/Model	Motor	Throat	Max. Cut	Blade Length	Min. Blade	Max. Blade	Weight (lbs.)
Craftsman 21461	$\frac{1}{2}$-hp	$9\frac{3}{8}"$	$5"$	$63\frac{1}{2}"$	$\frac{1}{4}"$	$\frac{3}{8}"$	91
Delta BS100	3-amp	$9"$	$3\frac{3}{4}"$	$59\frac{1}{2}"$	$\frac{1}{8}"$	$\frac{3}{8}"$	33
Delta BS150LS	$\frac{1}{2}$-hp	$10"$	$7"$	$72\frac{1}{2}"$	$\frac{1}{8}"$	$\frac{1}{2}"$	98
Delta BS220LS	$\frac{1}{2}$-hp	$12\frac{1}{4}"$	$6"$	$82"$	$\frac{1}{8}"$	$\frac{1}{2}"$	75
Grizzly 1052	$\frac{1}{2}$-hp	$9\frac{1}{4}"$	$4\frac{1}{8}"$	$64"$	$\frac{1}{8}"$	$\frac{1}{2}"$	100
Grizzly G8976	$\frac{1}{2}$-hp	$12"$	$3\frac{7}{8}"$	$62"$	$\frac{1}{4}"$	$\frac{3}{8}"$	38
Hitachi CB-13F	7-amp	$12"$	$5"$	$80"$	$\frac{1}{8}"$	$\frac{1}{2}"$	145
Jet JWBS-120	$\frac{1}{2}$-hp	$12"$	$6"$	$82"$	$\frac{1}{8}"$	$\frac{1}{2}"$	141
Ryobi BS1001SV	8-amp	$10"$	$4"$	$67"$	$\frac{1}{8}"$	$\frac{1}{2}"$	82

■ RECOMMENDATIONS

Floor-Model Band Saws

If space allows and you can afford it, we recommend a floor-model band saw—preferably a 14" saw with a closed stand. This saw will last a lifetime and will stand up to heavy use. Go with a name you can trust. Look for a band saw with smooth castings, a powerful motor ($1\frac{1}{2}$-hp), and an easy-to-change blade.

Make sure that replacement parts will be available in the future. (It's a good idea to actually order a couple of spare thrust bearings and guide blocks when you purchase your saw—they'll eventually fail, and you'll be glad you have them on hand.) Also, be sure that accessories like a rip fence and miter gauge either come standard with the saw or can be purchased from the manufacturer or a third-party accessory maker.

FLOOR MODEL BAND SAWS

Brand/Model	Motor	Throat	Max. Cut	Blade Length	Min. Blade	Max. Blade	Weight (lbs.)
Bridgewood PBS-440	3-hp	17"	12"	145"		1"	470
Bridgewood BW-17	2-hp	16$\frac{3}{16}$"	11$\frac{1}{4}$"	131$\frac{3}{4}$"	$\frac{1}{4}$"	1"	367
Bridgewood BW-14	1-hp	13$\frac{3}{8}$"	8"	100$\frac{7}{8}$"	$\frac{1}{4}$"	$\frac{3}{4}$"	202
Craftsman BAS300	$\frac{3}{4}$-hp	12"	6"	89$\frac{1}{2}$"	$\frac{1}{8}$"	$\frac{3}{4}$"	189
Craftsman BAS350	1-hp	13$\frac{5}{8}$"	6"	99$\frac{3}{4}$"	$\frac{1}{8}$"	$\frac{3}{4}$"	226
Delta 28-276	$\frac{3}{4}$-hp	13$\frac{3}{4}$"	6$\frac{1}{4}$"	93$\frac{1}{2}$"	$\frac{1}{4}$"	$\frac{3}{4}$"	201
Delta 28-248	1$\frac{1}{2}$-hp	13$\frac{3}{4}$"	6$\frac{1}{4}$"	93$\frac{1}{2}$"	$\frac{1}{4}$"	$\frac{3}{4}$"	224
Delta 28-682	2-hp	17$\frac{1}{2}$"	12"	136"	$\frac{1}{4}$"	1$\frac{1}{4}$"	397
General 490	1-hp	14$\frac{3}{4}$"	6$\frac{3}{4}$"	97$\frac{1}{2}$"	$\frac{1}{4}$"	$\frac{3}{4}$"	320
General 690	1$\frac{1}{2}$-hp	14$\frac{3}{4}$"	12$\frac{3}{4}$"	109$\frac{1}{2}$"	$\frac{1}{4}$"	$\frac{3}{4}$"	352
Grizzly G0555	1-hp	13$\frac{3}{8}$"	6"	92$\frac{1}{2}$"	$\frac{1}{8}$"	$\frac{3}{4}$"	167
Jet JWBS-14	1-hp	13$\frac{1}{2}$"	6"	93$\frac{1}{2}$"	$\frac{1}{8}$"	$\frac{3}{4}$"	185
Jet JWBS-16	1$\frac{1}{2}$-hp	16$\frac{3}{8}$"	10"	123"	$\frac{1}{8}$"	1$\frac{1}{4}$"	310
Jet JWBS-18	1$\frac{3}{4}$-hp	18$\frac{3}{8}$"	12$\frac{1}{4}$"	137"	$\frac{1}{8}$"	1$\frac{1}{2}$"	410
Laguna LT14SE	2-hp	13$\frac{1}{4}$"	12"	112"	$\frac{1}{16}$"	1"	242
Powermatic PWBS-14	1$\frac{1}{2}$-hp	13$\frac{1}{2}$"	6"	93$\frac{1}{2}$"	$\frac{1}{8}$"	$\frac{3}{4}$"	203

■ RECOMMENDATIONS

Industrial Band Saws

If your shop is large, your wallet is fat, and/or you simply need the added capacity an industrial band saw offers, go for it. These massive machines are a joy to use and will serve you well. Even the smaller versions are extremely well made and can handle tough cutting jobs (like resawing) that other saws couldn't even think about taking on. We are particularly impressed with the extremely well-engineered saw from Laguna Tools (www.lagunatools.com). They employ rigid metal frames, heavy-duty motors, and unique ceramic guide block systems (see page 31) that let you plow through even the toughest of woods.

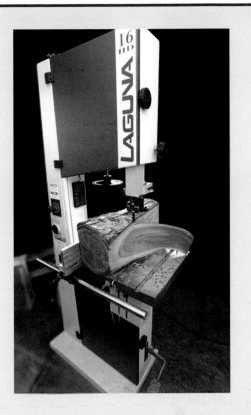

INDUSTRIAL BAND SAWS

Brand/Model	Motor	Throat	Max. Cut	Blade Length	Min. Blade	Max. Blade	Weight (lbs.)
Bridgewood PBS-540	5-hp	21"	14"	166"	1/4"	1 1/8"	602
Bridgewood PBS-740	6.6-hp	28"	19 1/2"	212"	1/4"	1 1/2"	1030
Craftsman 22450	2-hp	17 1/2"	10 3/4"	133"	3/16"	1"	280
Delta 28-640	2-hp	19"	11"	156 1/2"	1/4"	1"	585
Jet JWBS-20	2-hp	20"	12 1/4"	150"	1/8"	1 1/2"	596
Grizzly G0513	2-hp	16 1/4"	12"	131 1/2"	1/8"	1"	321
Grizzly G0514	2-hp	18 1/4"	12"	143"	1/8"	1 1/4"	383
Laguna LT16	3-hp	15 1/2"	12"	132"	1/16"	1"	352
Laguna LT16HD	4.5-hp	15"	16"	150"	1/16"	1 1/8"	465
Laguna LT18	4.5-hp	17"	18"	158"	1/18"	1 1/8"	473
Laguna LT20	4.5-hp	19"	20"	176"	1/8"	1 3/8"	564
Laguna LT24	4.5-hp	23 1/4"	24"	201"	1/8"	1 1/2"	755
Powermatic 2013	2-hp	20"	12 3/8"	158 1/2"	1/4"	1 1/2"	950
Powermatic 2415	2-hp	24 1/4"	14"	180 1/2"	1/4"	1 1/2"	1050

2 Band Saw Accessories

Unlike many other power tools, where you can spend a lot of money outfitting the tool with accessories, a band saw doesn't require a lot of fancy add-ons to do its job. The number one accessories you'll buy are blades. So it's important that you know all about blade selection, including length, width, profile, material, and set choices.

Other accessories worth mentioning are the various kinds of replacement guides available to help your blades run smooth and true, and an accurate rip fence for ripping, resawing, and joinery work. An item to note here: Although the number of accessories is small, some of their price tags can be large—in particular some of the guide systems and carbide-tipped blades that are available can easily run into the hundreds of dollars.

The three main accessories for a band saw are all shown here: various blades to handle a variety of cutting tasks, replacement guide blocks and guide systems to keep your blade in place, and a rip fence for ripping, resawing, and joint making.

Band Saw Blades

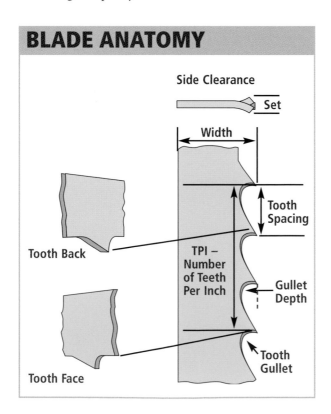

Band saw blades are available in many different types and blade profiles. They come in a wide variety of lengths and can also be custom-ordered to fit just about any saw. The standard length for a typical 14" band saw is 93 1/2".

Blade anatomy

A typical band saw blade is illustrated in the bottom left drawing. When selecting a blade, you'll need to specify its length, width, number of teeth per inch, set, and profile. Many band saw manufacturers only offer limited sizes and types, so it's good to know that blade makers offer much more. In particular, Lenox (www.lenoxsaw.com) and Olson Saw Company (www.olsonsaw.com) offer a wide range of quality band saw blades.

Blade length varies greatly from saw to saw, and it's important to check your owner's manual for the recommended size. Blade manufacturers stock blades for most of the standard band saws available and will also make blades to any length. Although it may seem expensive to have blades custom-made, it's not—they do this every day. In fact, some blade makers like Laguna Tools sell their blades by the inch. Blade widths vary from 1/16" up to 2", with 1/4", 3/8", 1/2", 3/4", and 1" being the most common—and readily available. Blade width is measured from the tips of the blade to the back edge of the blade, as illustrated in the bottom left drawing.

Teeth per inch

Next to blade length and width, you'll need to specify how many teeth per inch you want on your blade. Teeth per inch, or TPI, is measured from gullet to gullet, as illustrated in the bottom right drawing. Another less common way to specify tooth count is to call out the number of points per inch. This is measured from point to point and will always be one more than the number of teeth per inch. So a 4-TPI blade will have 5 points per inch. How many teeth a blade has per inch will impact the finish and feed rate. A coarse-toothed blade (2 to 4 TPI) is best used for resawing and cutting thick stock. Fine-toothed blades (above 18 TPI) are good for cutting thin metals and plastics. For most wood-cutting, blades that have 6 to 10 TPI work best. As a general rule of thumb, fewer teeth mean a fast but rough cut; more teeth provide a smoother cut, but at a slower feed rate.

BLADE ANATOMY

Side Clearance

Set

Width

Tooth Spacing

Tooth Back

TPI – Number of Teeth Per Inch

Gullet Depth

Tooth Face

Tooth Gullet

TEETH & POINTS PER INCH

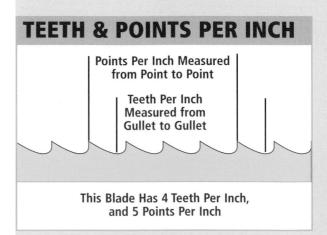

Points Per Inch Measured from Point to Point

Teeth Per Inch Measured from Gullet to Gullet

This Blade Has 4 Teeth Per Inch, and 5 Points Per Inch

COMMON BLADE PROFILES

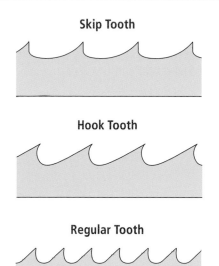

Skip Tooth

Hook Tooth

Regular Tooth

Tooth configurations

In addition to length, width, and teeth per inch, there are a couple of other things you'll need to specify when ordering a band saw blade. You'll also need to pick a tooth profile and the type of set (see page 28). Common profiles are skip tooth, hook tooth, and standard or regular profile, as illustrated in the top drawing.

For general-purpose work, we recommend a skip-tooth blade with a raker set. This style blade will handle most cutting jobs in the shop. For resawing, we recommend a hook-tooth blade, as it does a better job of clearing the kerf of sawdust (and there's a whole lot of that when resawing). Keeping the kerf clear will keep the blade cooler and running straighter..

DETERMINING BLADE LENGTH

In most cases, you can find the recommended blade length for your saw in your owner's manual. Alternatively, if you have the make and model number, you can contact the manufacturer or a blade manufacturer and they should be able to provide the length. For saws that are older and not in production anymore, neither of these may work and you'll have to figure out the length on your own. Here's how. Start by measuring the distance from the center of one wheel to the other. Then measure the diameter of one of the wheels at its widest point. Insert these two measurements in the equation shown in the drawing at right and do the math to determine the blade length. Note that it's important to have the wheel tension adjustment at its midpoint when you measure between the wheels, and not at one of its extremes. Measuring with the upper wheel at its midpoint provides room one way or the other to both fit the blade on the saw and tension it properly.

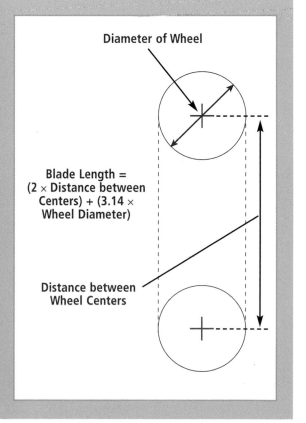

Diameter of Wheel

Blade Length =
(2 × Distance between Centers) + (3.14 × Wheel Diameter)

Distance between Wheel Centers

Blade set

There are three common ways band saw blades are set: alternate, raker, and wavy, as illustrated in the drawing below. Set is the amount each tooth is bent away from the saw blade. Without set, a blade would quickly bind in the kerf. Coarse-cutting blades generally have a wider set than finer-cutting blades. This allows for plenty of clearance between the blade and the wall of the kerf. Aggressively set teeth are also commonly used on blades intended to cut green or wet wood. Here again, the wider set provides much-needed chip clearance. On a raker-set blade, one tooth is set to the right, the next to the left, and the third (the raker) is not set. This set is useful for cutting thick stock, as the raker tooth helps keep the kerf clean. Alternate-set blades are good for general-purpose cutting and provide fast, smooth cuts. Wavy-set blades typically have small teeth and are used primarily for cutting metal.

Blade materials

Band saw blades come in three basic types: carbon steel, bi-metal, and carbide-tipped, as shown in the photo at right. Both the carbon steel and bi-metal blades work well, although the bi-metal blades tend to stay sharp longer. On a bi-metal blade, a thin strip of high-speed steel is laminated onto the blade body before the teeth are cut. These blades were developed for cutting metal and have found favor in woodworking shops, particularly those using large band saws and high feed rates. For the average woodworking shop, carbon steel blades work fine. Band saw blade thickness (not counting set) runs from 0.018" up to 0.035", with 0.025" and 0.032" being the most common. On quality blades the back (or main section of the blade) is hardened to RC 28–32 and the teeth themselves are hardened to RC 62–64. Hardening the teeth additionally creates blades that are very durable and can stand up to even the toughest sawing tasks.

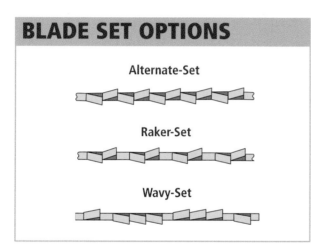

BLADE SET OPTIONS

Alternate-Set

Raker-Set

Wavy-Set

CARBIDE-TIPPED BLADES

Carbide-tipped blades are primarily used for cutting metal—a tough sawing task often associated with high feed rates. Carbide-tipped blades can also be used to take on tough wood-cutting jobs like resawing. Laguna Tools (www.lagunatools.com) makes a blade called the Resaw King, shown in the bottom photo. This blade has C-8 carbide steel tips welded onto a high-quality band. Then the teeth are ground to their finished thin-kerf profile with diamond grinders. The resulting blade cuts through even the thickest stock and leaves a surprisingly smooth surface. Resaw King blades are available in ¾", 1", 1⅜", and 2" widths. Their only downside is that they're expensive. A ¾"-wide blade for a standard 14" band saw will run well over $100. But if you do a lot of resawing, it's well worth the price.

Band saw welds

Band saw blades are made by cutting a blade to the desired length from a large spool and then welding the ends together. Because an overlapping splice would create a bump that would damage the guide blocks (and create a wider kerf), the ends of the splice are first ground to around 20-degree opposing angles before welding them together. Then the weld is ground smooth to match the thickness of the band, and any teeth at the weld need to be ground to the same profile as the other teeth on the blade.

Whenever you purchase a new band saw blade, it's always a good idea to inspect the weld before using the blade. The weld should be the same thickness as the band. If it's thicker, it'll create a ticking noise every time it passes the guide block. This is both annoying and damaging to the blocks. Also look to make sure the splice is well made and that the teeth are properly ground at the weld. Note the wider gullet and poorly shaped tooth at the weld on the lower blade compared to the upper blade in the top photo. If there are any weld issues, return the blade to the manufacturer for a replacement.

BLADE SELECTION CHART

Cutting Task	Teeth Per Inch	Blade Width	Blade Profile	Feed Rate
Crosscut (1" or less)	8–12	1/2" – 3/4"	Standard	Slow
Crosscut (1" or more)	6–10	1/2" – 3/4"	Standard	Slow
Curves (gradual)	6–12	1/4" – 3/8"	Skip	Medium
Curves (sharp)	10–14	1/8" – 1/4"	Standard	Slow
Mitering	8–14	1/2" – 3/4"	Standard	Slow/medium
Resawing	2–4	3/4" and up	Hook	Slow
Ripping (2" or less)	4–8	1/2" – 3/4"	Hook	Medium/fast
Ripping (2" or more)	2–6	1/2" – 3/4"	Hook	Slow/medium

Guide Blocks

As we mentioned earlier, the guide blocks or guide assemblies on a band saw are what keep the blade running true and prevent it from deflecting when cutting into a workpiece. Because this is such a critical part of the band saw, it's not too surprising that a number of band saw and accessory manufacturers have developed a variety of guide block materials and other systems to keep a blade on track. These include standard steel blocks, composite and ceramic guide blocks, roller-bearing and entire ceramic guide systems. You can even make your own guide blocks out of wood, as shown on the opposite page.

Steel

Steel guide blocks have been the standard for years. They're inexpensive and can be easily refaced on a grinder if they become scored, like the used set in the foreground of the photo at left (in the background is a new set of guide blocks). Many band saw manufacturers still ship their saws with steel guide blocks to keep manufacturing costs down. Steel blocks do an adequate job, but they have one main disadvantage: If your blade inadvertently hits them, they'll damage the blade. In the case of a carbide-tipped blade, this could mean broken tips.

Composite

The next step up from steel guide blocks are composite blocks, often sold under the brand name Cool Blocks. These blocks are made of graphite-impregnated phenolic laminate, as shown in the top right photo. The graphite is a synthetic dry lubricant that keeps the blade running smooth without making it oily. Unlike steel blocks that can generate friction and heat when they contact the blade, there's no metal-to-metal contact with composite blocks, so your blades will run cooler and smoother and will last longer. This means that you can adjust the blocks so they touch the blade—something that's very useful when using 1/16" or 1/8" blades. Conventional steel blocks cannot support these narrower blades without ruining them.

Ceramic

Guide blocks made of ceramic have been used in the sawmill industry for years. One leading manufacturer of these, Spaceage Ceramic Guideblocks (www.spaceageceramicguideblocks.com), offers ceramic guide blocks for many of the more common woodworking band saws, as shown in the bottom right photo. These blocks create less friction than steel, so the blade will run cooler and therefore last longer than a blade supported by steel guide blocks. Just like composite blocks, you can adjust ceramic blocks very close to the blade without fear of damaging the blade.

Ball bearings

Another way to reduce harmful friction between the blade and the guides is to replace the guide blocks with ball bearings, as shown in the top photo. This way if the blade contacts the bearing, it rotates, and minimal friction and heat is created. Most band saw manufacturers, as well as Carter Products (www.carterproducts.com), offer bearing guide upgrade kits. These kits typically include a set of upper and lower mounting brackets and the necessary hardware for a wide variety of band saws. (See pages 160–161 for more on installing ball-bearing guides.)

Wooden

An inexpensive alternative to composite blocks is to make your own out of wood. Although wood guide blocks can wear quickly, they can be resurfaced in seconds and will not harm your blade if contact is made. The blocks shown here are cut from teak, which is a naturally oily wood. (For more on making your own guide blocks, see pages 138–139.)

LAGUNA GUIDES

The folks at Laguna Tools (www.lagunatools.com) offer guide sets that employ ceramic for both the guide blocks and the thrust bearing, as shown in the bottom left photo. These guides provide superior performance, as the guides support the blade above and below the back blade guide (which replaces the thrust bearing). This prevents the blade from twisting during a cut and provides superb blade stability.

Kit. A Laguna guide kit consists of an upper and lower guide assembly. Each assembly holds five ceramic blocks: two upper, two lower, and a back blade guide. Laguna offers kits for the more common woodworking band saws.

Installed on a saw. As you can see in the photo, the Laguna guides support the blade above and below the back bearing guide. The guides are easy to install and a joy to use.

Dust Collection

A band saw can create an amazing amount of really fine dust—especially when resawing or cutting thick wood. To protect your lungs and help keep your shop clean, we recommend you use some form of dust collection with your saw. Dust collection will also keep your saw cleaner and running smoother longer. Most band saws now offer built-in dust pick-ups that make it easy to connect to a shop vacuum or dust collector. Some even offer built-in dust collection, like the Ryobi saw shown in the photo below. Even with these pick-ups the saw will still generate dust, so it's important to also wear a dust mask. Additionally, you can enhance your dust collection with the supplementary shop-made pick-up illustrated in the bottom right drawing.

pop out due to vibration. A strip of duct tape will prevent this from happening. If your shop vacuum hose doesn't fit the built-in pick-up, check with the vacuum manufacturer to see if they sell adapters. If they don't, you can usually fabricate one yourself from PVC pipe and fittings.

Shop-made pick-up

The band saw pick-up illustrated in the bottom drawing is meant to supplement the main pick-up of the saw, not replace it. On a band saw, much of the dust is collected by a dust port located near the bottom of the case. But it doesn't capture all the dust. The pick-up shown here attaches to the band saw table and reaches in via a length of PVC pipe to capture the dust thrown out by the gullets of the blade. You'll need to use trial and error to find the best location to attach the support block and to determine the length of the pipe. You want to get the pipe as close to the blade as possible without interfering with the blade, guide blocks, or thrust bearing. Once you've determined the length of the pipe, add 2³/₄" so it can pass through the support block and protrude enough to attach a flexible hose.

Built-in collection

The Ryobi saw shown in the above photo offers built-in dust collection. Suction is provided via a radial fan incorporated into the lower saw wheel. This pulls dust down and away from the blade and pushes it out through a dust bag, which filters out and stores the dust. What's really nice about this setup is that there is no vacuum or dust collector noise—just the sound of the saw running.

Standard pick-ups

The pick-ups built into most band saws are designed to accept the standard 1¹/₄" hose adapter commonly found on most shop vacuums, as shown in the top right photo. These generally slip into place, but can

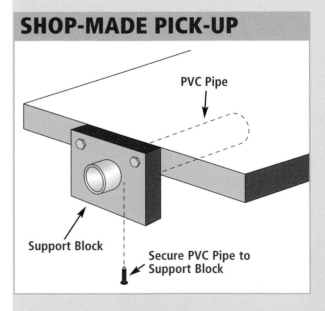

SHOP-MADE PICK-UP

PVC Pipe

Support Block

Secure PVC Pipe to Support Block

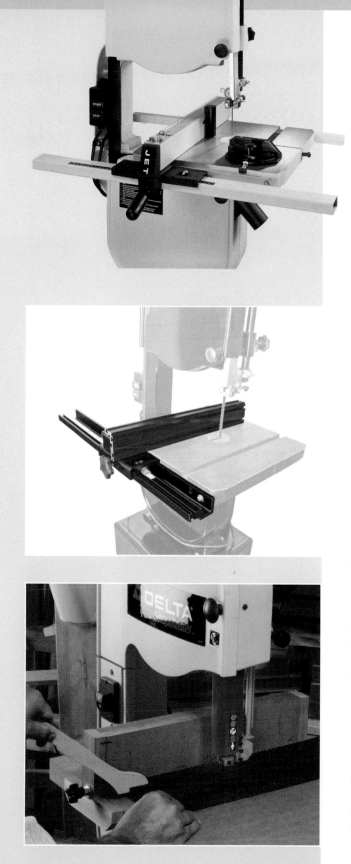

Rip Fences

When many woodworkers think about a band saw, they think about cutting curves. But a band saw also excels at ripping (see page 51–52) and joint making (see pages 81–89). For any of these operations, you'll need a rip fence. Your saw may have come with one, or you can add one made by an accessory manufacturer, or you can build your own.

Manufacturer-supplied

The manufacturer of your saw may include a rip fence with your saw, or it may be available as an added accessory. Most rip fences ride on a rail or rails attached to the saw table, as shown in the top photo. Quality fences will glide smoothly over the rails and have an easy-to-use positive lock. Many incorporate a tape measure on the front rail that's good for roughly positioning the fence. The fence itself should be flat, straight, and smooth and be adjustable to compensate for drift (see page 52).

Aftermarket

There are a number of add-on or aftermarket fences available that fit the most common brands of band saws. The fence system shown in the middle photo is manufactured by Kreg Tool Co. (www.kregtool.com). Their system includes a fence that's adjustable in two dimensions for ease in setting it parallel to the blade. Cutting accuracy and repeatability is further enhanced by the lens curser that reads off of the scale attached to the front rail.

Shop-built

If you like the idea of a rip fence but don't want to spend the money to buy one, consider making your own. Although you can simply clamp any straight piece of wood to the saw table to act as a fence, this can be quite frustrating, as the underside of the band saw table is not smooth and clamping can be a real challenge. An alternative solution is to make the table and fence system shown in the bottom photo and described in detail on pages 99–111.

Fence Accessories

A rip fence all by itself is a useful accessory. But you can increase its versatility by adding one or more fence accessories like a micro-adjuster, a resaw guide, and a stop.

Micro-adjusters

Some of the accessory fences available can be fitted with a micro-adjuster. These are particularly useful when cutting joinery. A micro-adjuster like the one shown in the top photo and manufactured by Kreg Tool Co. (www.kregtool.com) attaches to the rip fence and clamps onto the front rail. By turning the knurled knob on the micro-adjuster you can dial in the exact position of the fence. Then simply lock the rip fence in place. Need to readjust? Loosen the rip fence lock and fine-tune to the desired spot.

Resaw guide

Kreg Tool Co. also offers a resaw guide for their rip fence system as shown in the middle photo. The guide features a curved front face that provides plenty of support when resawing on the fly, to correct for drift. The adjustable guide attaches to the rip fence via a set of bolts that fit into slots in the fence. Knurled knobs connect to the bolts so you can position the guide exactly where you want it.

Stops

You can be more precise when cutting joints on the band saw by adding a stop to the fence. A stop limits how far the blade cuts into the workpiece. A simple stop can be clamped to the fence to stop or limit the workpiece. A more elegant alternative is to add an adjustable stop to your fence like the one shown in the bottom photo and described on pages 108–109. This stop is held in place via a bolt that passes through the fence. Although it was designed to work with the shop-built fence described on pages 103–107, it can be adapted to work with virtually any fence.

Band Saw Jigs and Add-Ons

In addition to a rip fence and fence accessories, there are a couple of other noteworthy jigs and add-ons you can purchase for your band saw. These include a circle-cutting jig, a featherboard, wheel brushes, and a blade stabilizer.

Circle-cutting jig

With a circle-cutting jig, you can cut perfect circles on the band saw. At its simplest, a circle-cutting jig provides a pin that serves as a pivot point to rotate a workpiece into the saw blade. On better jigs, this pin can be adjusted to create a wide range of circles. The circle jig shown in the top photo is manufactured by Woodhaven (www.woodhaven.com) and is designed as an accessory to their rip fence. The jig allows you to cut circles up to 28" in diameter. Alternatively, you can make your own; see pages 112–117.

Featherboards

If your saw table has a slot for a miter gauge, there are a number of accessory manufacturers that make featherboards that ride in this slot, as shown in the photo at right.

Bench Dog Tools (www.benchdog.com) sells one called Feather-Loc that fits in standard miter gauge slots (3/4" wide by 3/8" deep) found on many band saws. A featherboard presses stock firmly against the rip fence for more accurate cuts. You can also make your own (see pages 92–93). For a unique shop-made vertical featherboard that's perfect for resawing, see pages 94–95.

Wheel brushes

A set of wheel brushes (like those shown in the top right photo) are an inexpensive and quick way to improve the performance of your band saw. Wheel brushes mount inside the saw case so they contact the wheels to provide constant cleaning action. Keeping your saw wheels free from built-up pitch, sap, and dust allows your blades to track better, which results in more accurate cuts.

Blade stabilizer

In addition to the quality bearing guide systems that Carter Products (www.carterproducts.com) makes, they also manufacture an accessory called a blade stabilizer (inset photo at right) that provides excellent stability when cutting with blades 1/4" or less in width. The stabilizer fits into the slot normally occupied by your saw's side support block holder, and your blade fits into a groove machined into the surface of the bearing. Carter makes a blade stabilizer to fit most saws, and these can be attached to the band saw guide in seconds.

3 Basic Band Saw Techniques

The band saw is an incredibly versatile cutting machine. In this chapter, we'll cover the basics so you can get started making sawdust. We'll start with changing a blade, as this is a fundamental skill that with practice can take only a few minutes. Then we'll move on to setting up to cut and cover the basic safety rules, including when and how to use push sticks, push blocks, and featherboards.

The basic techniques of crosscutting and ripping are then covered, as well as curve-cutting tips. We'll show you how to work with long stock and how to cut narrow and thin stock, as well as how to work safely with small pieces. Finally, we'll cover cutting round stock and working with non-wood materials like metal, plastic, and composites.

The band saw is an "I can't make this cut on any other saw" kind of tool. Band saws excel at cutting curves, ripping, crosscutting, and making stopped cuts as shown here.

Changing Blades

To get the most out of your band saw, it's important to match the blade to the cutting task. (For more on blade selection, see the chart on page 29.) Resawing requires a wide blade with few teeth per inch; intricate cuts call for narrow blades and more teeth per inch. We've known a lot of woodworkers—even experienced ones—who leave a 1/4" 7- to 10-TPI blade on their saw and use it to make all cuts because they don't want to hassle with changing blades.

That's too bad, because although you can make a lot of cuts with a 1/4" blade, you'll end up with poor-quality surfaces (rough and torn wood fibers) on many of your project parts. Additionally, using a blade like this to cut heavy stock or to resaw will shorten the blade's life since it's not designed for this kind of work. It'll also likely dull the blade, producing even rougher cuts. That's why it's so important to get in the habit of changing blades as needed. With time, you'll be able to change a blade and make all the necessary adjustments in just a couple of minutes. Yes, it will take longer in the beginning, but if you follow the sequence described here, changing blades will become an almost effortless task.

Raise the guard

To change a blade on a band saw, start by raising the upper guide assembly and guard as high as it will go, as shown in the bottom left photo. This provides better access to the insert plate in the saw table (which can be removed now) and lets you see the lower guide assembly. If necessary, you may need to remove the guard (inset photo above) to get the blade off; check your owner's manual to see whether or not this is necessary.

Remove the covers

Next, to access the blade and saw wheels, remove or open the covers for the upper and lower sections of the saw as shown in the top right photo.

Back off the guides and thrust bearings

Although this next step may seem unnecessary, it'll save you from damaging a new blade. Whenever we go to change a blade, we start by backing off both sets of guide blocks and the thrust bearings on the upper and the lower guide assemblies, as shown in the middle photos.

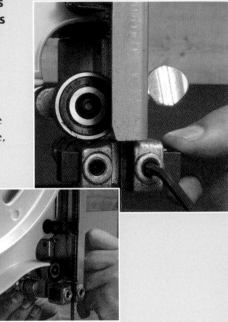

This does two things: It makes removing and replacing the blade easier, and it also prevents damage to your new blade as you adjust tracking—that is, how the blade rides on the wheels. All blades track slightly different on the wheels, and if you leave the guides in place, there's a good chance the sharpened blade tips will strike the guide blocks, dulling them. Besides, when you track a blade, it's best to see how it runs on the wheels without any kind of guide or interference.

Remove the table pin and/or front rail

When it's time to remove the blade, you'll need to pull it out through the slot in the saw table. All saws have some sort of device to keep the split sections of the table aligned. The most common device is a table pin like that shown in the top photo. Although these don't have threads—they're actually just tapered pins—you'll find the easiest way to remove one is by rotating the pin with a wrench to ease it out of the tapered hole in the top. Other saw tables employ a nut and bolt. Note that depending on the location of the slot in the top, you may need to temporarily remove the front rail if a rip fence is used.

Release the blade tension

Now you can release the tension on the blade. On the Delta saw shown in the middle photo, this is just a matter of pulling the quick-release lever forward. On most other saws, you'll need to turn the tension-adjustment knob until the blade is loose enough to be removed.

Remove the blade

At this point you can remove the blade. Since you've backed off the guide blocks and thrust bearings, and the blade guard and table pin have been removed, this should be a snap. Just lift the blade carefully off the wheels and rotate it if needed so it'll fit into the slot in the saw top, as shown in the bottom left photo. Guide the blade out of the slot, fold the blade (as shown on page 42), and set it aside. Now is the perfect time to clean the wheels. We keep old toothbrushes around the shop for jobs like this. Just scrub the wheel tires as you slowly rotate each wheel, as shown in the bottom inset photo.

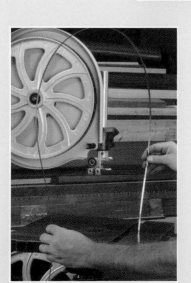

Install the new blade

Now you're ready for the new blade. Remove it from its packaging and unfold it. Check the orientation of the teeth to make sure they'll be pointing down as they run through the guide assemblies, and thread the blade through the slot in the saw table and position it on the wheels so it's centered on the width of the wheels, as shown in the top photo.

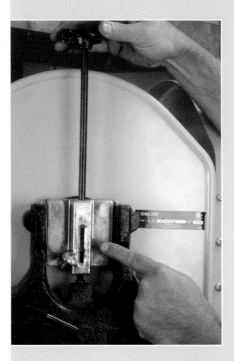

Adjust the tension

With the new blade in place, gradually increase the tension by turning the tension knob as shown in the middle photo. Most manufacturers have a tension indicator inside the saw's case or on the exterior (as shown here). This indicator is calibrated to match the width of the blade. So simply crank the knob until the tension indicator matches your blade width. Depending on the age of your saw—and the condition of your tension spring—you may find that it's necessary to adjust the tension to the next wider blade width to achieve satisfactory results. (For more on tension adjustments and problems caused by insufficient tension, see page 169.)

Adjust the tracking

After the blade is tensioned, you can check to see how it tracks on the wheels and adjust this if necessary. Give the top wheel a spin (we recommend using a short length of dowel for this—it's easy to pinch your fingers) to see whether the blade is tracking correctly; that is, it remains centered on the wheels. If it doesn't, loosen the tracking lock knob or wing nut and adjust the tracking (as shown in the bottom photo) until the blade tracks evenly.

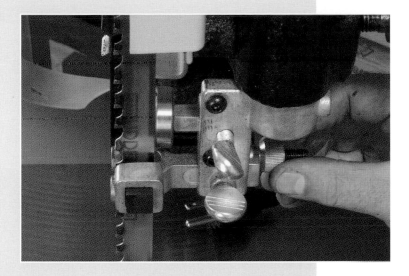

Position the upper guide assembly

Now that the blade is installed, tensioned properly, and tracking true, you can adjust the upper and lower guide assemblies. For starters, you'll need to position each assembly so the guide blocks can do their job. All guide assemblies move forward and back with respect to the front edge of the saw table. On some saws (like the Delta 14" saw shown in the top photo) there's a convenient thumbscrew lock and a knurled knob that when turned moves the assembly in and out. What you're looking for here is to position the guide blocks so that they will support the blade as much as possible without ever making contact with the blade's teeth. Repeat this adjustment for the lower guide assembly.

Adjust the thrust bearings

The purpose of the thrust bearing is to prevent the workpiece from forcing the blade off the wheels during a cut. Basically, the blade butts up against it and can't go back any farther. Because it's a bearing, it spins as the blade rubs up against it—and this keeps the blade from scoring the bearing. To prevent excess wear of the bearing, it should be adjusted so it only contacts the blade when stock is being cut. If you slip a dollar bill between the blade and the bearing and adjust for a snug fit, you'll have the correct clearance, as shown in the middle photo.

Adjust the guide blocks

How you adjust the guide blocks will depend on your saw and the type of guide blocks. Metal blocks and bearing systems should be adjusted to within 0.004" of the blade. This happens to be the thickness of U.S. paper currency, which works as a nifty feeler gauge. Just wrap a bill around the blade and press the guide blocks in for a snug fit and tighten them in place, as shown in the bottom photo. Make sure when you press the guide blocks in place that you do not cause the blade to deflect or bow in either direction.

Adjust the lower guide assembly

After you've adjusted the upper guide assembly, go ahead and repeat this procedure for the lower guide assembly. Start by positioning the guide blocks from front to back and then for the correct gap, as shown in the top photo. Note that on many saws, space is quite cramped below the table and it may be easier to make your adjustments through the blade opening in the saw top, as shown here.

Pulse the power

Now give the blade a quick "pulse" test to make sure everything is aligned properly. As quick as you can, turn the power on and off for just a second. This brief dynamic test can save a lot of blades, guides, and thrust bearings. This is much safer than simply turning on the saw and letting it run. If the blade is over-tensioned and prone to breakage, it's best to have it happen with a pulse versus full power.

If all looks good, turn on the saw and let it run a minute as so. Fine-tune any adjustments as needed. Quite often you'll find that the blade tracks differently under power and is contacting one or both thrust bearings. If you see either bearing spinning,

stop the saw and back the bearing away from the blade. The only time thrust bearings should spin is during a cut when the blade bows backward slightly from pressure exerted by the workpiece. Finish up by installing the table pin, fence (if necessary), and saw top insert, as shown in the bottom photo.

FOLDING A BLADE

Folding a blade looks complicated but really isn't, after you've done it a couple of times. Consider practicing with an old blade (as illustrated in the drawing at right) until you get the hang of it.

Once folded, store the blade properly (for more on blade storage, see page 146).

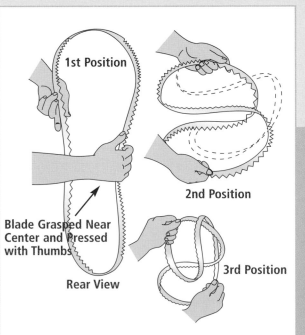

1st Position

2nd Position

Blade Grasped Near Center and Pressed with Thumbs

Rear View

3rd Position

Working with Patterns

Many of the parts you'll be cutting to shape with a band saw will require a pattern. There are a number of ways to transfer a pattern to a workpiece, including spray adhesive, carbon and tracing paper, and heat transfer. We'll also share some tips here for working with patterns.

Spray adhesive

There are a couple of advantages to spray-on adhesive: It goes on fast, the coating is typically uniform and even (as long as you don't pause in one spot as you spray), and the adhesive holds well. It's important to spray on a light coat (as shown in the top photo), or you can end up scraping the paper off the wood once you're done cutting. It's also a good idea to clear the nozzle after each use to prevent it from clogging. Just hold the can upside down and press the nozzle down until just air comes out.

Carbon and tracing paper

With the advent of computers and printers capable of spewing out multiple copies of a document, good old-fashioned carbon paper is getting harder to find these days. It still works great, though. Just slip a piece of it between the pattern and the workpiece (as shown in the middle photo) and trace the pattern. A ballpoint pen works best for tracing—especially the roller-ball type—as it slides effortlessly across the pattern with little risk of tearing the pattern. Tracing paper is also excellent for duplicating patterns. This tissue-thin material does have a tendency to tear easily, so it's best to use a felt-tip marker for tracing, as it will reduce the risk of tearing.

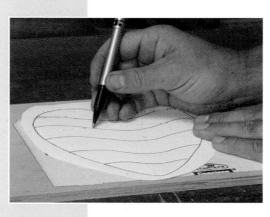

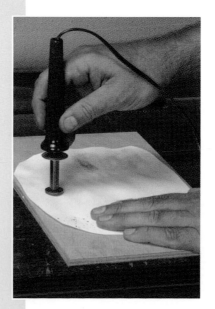

Direct transfer using heat

If the patterns you're using for a project were made on a copy machine, there's one other technique you can use to transfer the pattern to the workpiece—heat. Because the toner used to make the pattern copy is heat-sensitive, you can reheat it and it will melt and fuse to the workpiece. For years, woodworkers have used a standard household iron for this. But now there are specialty transfer tools for this. A transfer tool looks like a small soldering iron, but instead of a pointed tip, it has a flat, smooth tip about the size of a quarter. After allowing the tool to heat up the recommended time, all you do is place the pattern on the workpiece with the printed side down and press the transfer tool against the pattern as shown in the bottom photo. The type of wood and the darkness of the copy will determine how fast or slow you need to move the transfer tool. As a general rule, if you see the paper discolor slightly, the pattern has been successfully transferred.

Group layout

One technique that can save you money when working with patterns or templates is to group your patterns to conserve stock. When grain direction isn't an issue, you can rotate and flop patterns or templates as needed to get them close together, as shown in the top photo. This is something that's not as easily done when you use a paper pattern unless you go to the trouble of cutting out the pattern.

Grain direction and starting/ending cuts

How you start a cut into a work-piece can impact how easy or hard it is to follow the pattern. Whenever you start with the grain, you run the risk of the blade following the grain. In most cases, you'll find it easier to control if you start your cuts against the grain, as shown in the middle photo.

Plastic templates

A final tip for working with patterns and templates is instead of using hardboard to make a template, use thin plastic. A thin plastic template, like the one shown in the bottom photo, lets the grain show through so you can move the template around as desired to get the best color and grain pattern. (For more on working with plastic, see page 61.)

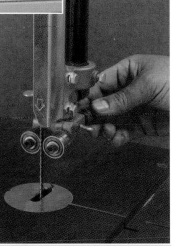

Setting Up to Cut

Whenever you go to use a stationary power tool, it's a good idea to go through a set routine—much like a pre-flight check that pilots do—before turning on the tool. With a band saw, this includes changing a blade if necessary to match the cut you're about to make, and adjusting the guide blocks or thrust bearing and blade tension; it also means protecting yourself and setting up to cut accurately and safely.

Change the blade if necessary

As we mentioned earlier, to get the best performance from your saw, it's important to match the blade to the task at hand. If you're about to resaw, take the time to switch to a wider blade; for intricate cuts, switch to a narrower blade. Likewise if the cutting task requires more tension, adjust the tension as needed as shown in the top photo.

Adjust blocks and/or thrust bearings

Even if you haven't changed the blade, take a moment to inspect the guides and thrust bearings to make sure they're adjusted properly. Quite frequently, a blade will track differently over time, and if you're not careful, it can creep forward until it strikes the guides. Check the guides for the correct gap, and position and adjust accordingly, as shown in the middle photo.

Adjust upper guide position

You'll also want to adjust the position of the upper guide to match the thickness of your workpiece, as shown in the bottom photo. In general, you want the guide assembly as close as possible to the surface of the workpiece without causing binding. A 1/8" gap between the workpiece and the bottom of the upper guide assembly works well.

Eye/ear/dust protection.
Any cut you make on the band saw will create noise, sawdust, and debris. That's why it's so important to protect yourself when sawing. Small bench-top band saws in particular make a lot of noise—those with universal motors tend to really whine—so keep a set of earmuffs within easy reach and wear them religiously, along with eye protection and a dust mask to keep dust from entering your eyes and lungs, as shown in the top photo.

■ BAND SAW SAFETY RULES

1. Read the instruction manual that came with your saw from cover to cover, and follow all safety rules.
2. Use certified safety equipment: eye, hearing, and dust protection.
3. Dress properly: Don't wear ties, gloves, or loose clothing; remove all jewelry.
4. Never use a power saw in wet or damp locations.
5. Maintain your saw in peak condition; see Chapter 6 for more on this.
6. Before using your saw, check for damaged parts and make repairs as needed.
7. Keep your work area clean and uncluttered.
8. Keep children, pets, and visitors away when operating the saw.
9. Always use the guard and push stick or push blocks whenever possible.
10. Listen to your "safety sense." If a cut seems dangerous, it probably is; stop and rethink the cut.
11. Never use force to make a cut. If force is needed, something is wrong; stop the saw and find out what's not right.
12. Turn off the saw and unplug it before changing blades or accessories.
13. Never leave a saw running unattended; turn it off if you need to walk away from it.
14. Use dust collection if possible, to protect your lungs and reduce dust in the shop.

15. Change the saw blade as needed to match the cutting task.
16. Never start a band saw before clearing the saw table of all objects.
17. Never start the saw with the blade in contact with a workpiece.
18. Hold the workpiece firmly, and feed it into the blade at a moderate speed.
19. Turn the saw off before attempting to back out of an uncompleted or jammed cut.
20. Check the blade tension regularly and carefully. This helps prevent blade breakage.
21. Use a holding device for small workpieces.
22. Don't force material through the saw; it can cause binding of the workpiece. Do not force curved cuts with too small a radius for the width of blade being used; this will also cause unnecessary binding and possible blade breakage.
23. Keep your hands away from the blade. Use a push-stick to free the work. Never place your fingers in line with the blade.
24. Allow the blade to come to a complete stop before removing scrap stock from the table. Be attentive to thin cut-off pieces hitting the end of the slot in the insert, or jamming in the slot.

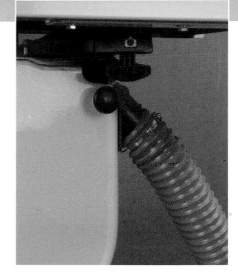

Hook up dust collection

A dust mask will keep dust out of your lungs, but not out of the shop. We strongly recommend that you connect a shop vacuum or dust collection system to your saw whenever you use it, as shown in the top photo.
Most bench-top and stationary band saws (like the one shown here) have a convenient port on the side that accepts the hose connector of the standard shop vacuum.

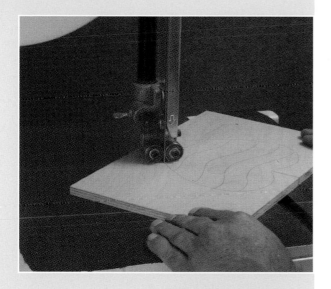

Hand position

Proper hand position when using the band saw is one of the best habits you can get into to prevent accidents. When possible, keep your hands on the extremities of the workpiece, as far away from the blade as possible, as shown in the middle photo. It's also a good idea to guide the workpiece with your fingers, with the palms of your hands resting on the table, as shown here. This creates a foundation for movement that helps prevent jerky motions that can lead to both sloppy cuts and accidents.

Check blade for perpendicular to table

Finally, it's always a good idea to check to make sure that your saw's table is perpendicular to the blade before making a cut. With use, a band saw table can creep out of alignment. Keep a small engineer's square or combination square handy (like the one shown in the bottom photo) to check the table before you cut, and adjust the table if needed to bring it into square.

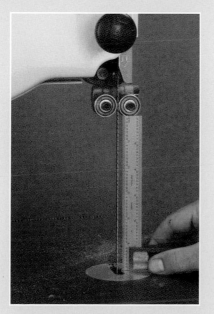

◼ PREVENTING COLUMN INTERFERENCE

Unlike other power saws, the structure of a band saw itself can prevent you from making the desired cut. We're talking about the column or frame of the saw and how this limits the cut you can make—basically, the throat depth. This may seem obvious if you want to cut to the center of a 36"-wide panel and you've got a 14" band saw. What isn't readily apparent is the problems the column can cause when you want to make crosscuts in a long piece. Fortunately, there are a number of ways to get around this.

Angled cuts. If you need to crosscut a board that's longer than your throat depth, angle the board as shown in the top photo. Then once the board is cut in two, you can go back and cut the end square. Yes, this does waste wood, but it allows you to make the cut.

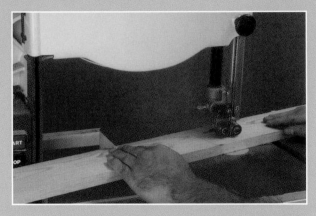

Mark both sides. Another way to work around the column is to mark both sides of a workpiece for cutting. Notice that in the middle photo that the column interferes with the cut. But when you mark both sides of the workpiece, you can flip the workpiece so the column doesn't interfere, as shown in the middle inset photo.

Backtracking. Finally, if you do encounter interference from the column as shown in the bottom photo, turn off the saw and back out of the cut. Then attack the cut from a different angle as shown in the bottom inset photo. Frequently this is all you need to do to complete a cut. If this doesn't work, consider marking both sides of the workpiece as described above.

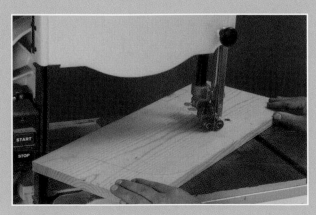

Using Safety Devices

One of the most reliable ways to keep your fingers away from the sharp blade of a band saw is to use a safety device such as a push stick, push block, or featherboard, as described below.

Push stick

Push sticks come in wide variety of shapes and sizes. You can purchase them or make your own. The push stick shown in the top photo is easy to make and readily replaced if it happens to hit the blade. It can be made from $1/2$"- or $3/4$"-thick scrap stock. Solid wood is fine, but plywood with its cross-banded layers will prove to be stronger over time. For a pattern for this push stick, see page 98.

Push block

Although push blocks are most often used with table saws and jointers, they can come in handy when resawing. Instead of using the push block in the traditional horizontal position, the push block is held vertically as shown in the middle photo. This way you can feed stock into the blade when resawing and keep your fingers completely out of harm's way.

Featherboard

A featherboard has a set of flexible fingers at its end. When clamped against a workpiece, these fingers press the workpiece firmly into the rip fence to ensure an accurate cut. You can buy featherboards or make one yourself. The shop-made version shown in the bottom photo is designed to slide back and forth in the miter gauge slot, and locks in place with a simple home-made clamp system. It's adjustable to handle a variety of stock widths and is both easy to make and easy to use. (For detailed directions on how to make this featherboard, see pages 92–93.)

Straight Crosscuts

Generally, longer boards are broken down into shorter lengths. The workpiece is pushed past the blade either freehand or with the aid of the miter gauge that fits in the slot or track cut into the saw table.

Freehand crosscuts

In cases where you simply want to crosscut a workpiece and aren't concerned about accuracy, you can use your hand as a miter gauge. Just slip your thumb into the miter gauge slot as shown in the top photo and grip the workpiece. To make the cut, turn on the saw and slide your hand forward while keeping a solid grip on the workpiece. Since the edges of miter gauge slots are often rough, make sure to file these before trying this technique as described on page 142.

Using the miter gauge

Most likely you will want your crosscuts to be precise, and this calls for a miter gauge as shown in the middle photo. The key to making precise crosscuts is making sure the miter gauge is adjusted so it's perfectly perpendicular to the blade (see page 144). Also, the heads of most miter gauges are quite short (typically 5" to 7" in length). This does not provide adequate support for most crosscuts. To better support a workpiece for a crosscut,

attach a wood auxiliary fence to the body of the miter gauge. There are holes in the body of most miter gauges just for this purpose. If you extend the fence an inch or two past the saw blade, it will also support the cut-off and prevent tear-out. Finally, to prevent your workpiece from "creeping" or shifting during the cut, apply a piece of sandpaper to the face of the auxiliary fence or to the head of the miter gauge. The grit of the paper will help grip the workpiece.

Crosscutting wide workpieces

Occasionally, you'll need to crosscut a wide workpiece where you can't use the miter gauge. In cases like this you'd have to pull the miter gauge so far out from the saw table that the bar on the miter gauge wouldn't engage the slot in the saw table. To get around this, simply reverse the miter gauge as shown in the bottom photo. Just make sure to butt the workpiece firmly up against the head of the miter gauge as you make your cut.

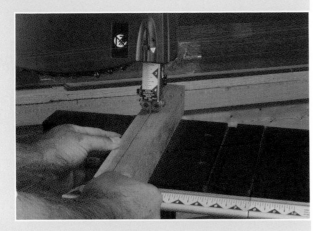

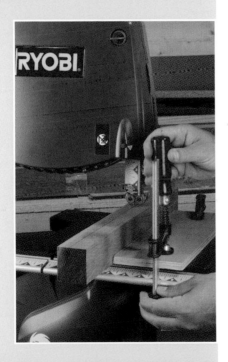

Straight Ripping

Although the band saw is known primarily as a curve-cutting machine, it does a surprisingly good job of making straight cuts. It's particularly useful for ripping short stock that would be unsafe to cut on the table saw. If you plan on using your rip fence as a guide, it's important that you first check for drift and compensate for any if necessary.

Checking for drift

Blade drift is caused by unevenly set teeth. An uneven set tends to pull a workpiece one way or the other as it cuts. You can try to fight this, but you'll lose. You'll be better off identifying the drift and then compensating for it by angling the rip fence. To check for drift, start by striking a line along the length of a scrap of wood. Then turn on the saw and cut about halfway through the piece, taking care to follow the line regardless of how much or which way you have to angle the workpiece to do this, as shown in the top photo.

Compensating for drift

Now turn off the saw, making sure not to move the workpiece. The angle of the workpiece matches the drift caused by the blade. There are a couple of ways to compensate for drift. Some rip fences are adjustable and can by angled as needed. If you're using a simple wood fence clamped to the saw table as shown in the middle photo, you'll need to angle the fence to match the workpiece. Alternatively, you can draw a pencil line on the saw top to match the angle of the workpiece and then set up your fence so it's parallel to this line.

Ripping freehand

If you're freehand-cutting a workpiece (that is, you're not using the fence), you may want to raise the guard about 1/4" above the workpiece—this makes it easier to see the cut line. Turn on the saw and push the workpiece into the cut as shown in the bottom photo. As you near the end of the cut, switch to a push stick to guide it safely past the blade.

Ripping using a fence

Once you've checked and compensated for drift (if necessary), you can rip your workpiece. Just slide the fence over to the desired width and lock or clamp it in place. Turn on the saw and push the workpiece into the blade, taking care to switch to a push stick as you near the end of the cut.

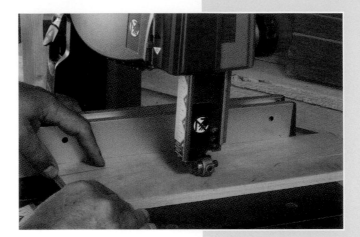

Pushing/pulling stock

If you don't have a push stick handy, you can also safely finish the cut by pushing and pulling it past the blade as shown in the middle photo. If you use this technique, make sure to keep the edge of the workpiece firmly pressed up against the rip fence as you finish the cut.

RIP FENCE EXTENDER FOR NARROW RIPS

If you need to rip either thin stock or a narrow piece, you'll discover that you can't lower the upper guide assembly down as far as you want because it'll hit the rip fence when it's positioned near the blade. To remedy this unsafe situation, use an auxiliary fence to extend the rip fence far enough away from the blade so you can safely lower the guide assembly as shown in the bottom photo. The extender is just a pair of scraps glued together to form an "L" and clamped to the rip fence as shown.

Curved Cuts

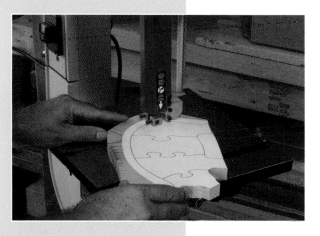

Curved cuts are easy on the band saw; just make sure that you know the radius limitations of the blade, as illustrated on page 54.

Basic technique

Cutting curves is what a band saw is all about. To make a curved cut, guide the workpiece with both hands as shown in the top photo. There are a couple of different techniques you can use to cut a smooth curve. With one method, you leave one hand fixed and push the edge of the workpiece with the other to pivot the workpiece into the blade. This will create a smooth-flowing curve. The problem is it's hard to know when to pivot the workpiece—only time spent at the saw will help you develop this skill. The other method is to keep both hands moving to guide the workpiece and make the cut. This is more common, but generally produces a rougher curve.

Gentle curves are a snap to cut, as it's just a matter of following your cut line. For circle cuts, try pressing down near the center of the workpiece and rotate the workpiece into the blade—you can get a surprisingly accurate circle this way. Alternatively, you can use a circle jig as described on page 35 and pages 112–117.

"Nibbling" or filing with the blade

One technique that most experienced band saw users have picked up over time is to use a saw blade as a "file" to clean up cuts and remove bumps or ridges. This requires a light touch, but can be very useful. To file with a blade, gently push the workpiece into the blade at the point where you want to clean up—if necessary, wiggle the workpiece from side to side to help file a smooth transition, as shown in the bottom photo.

Breaking up curves with relief cuts

For tight curves, you may find it necessary to cut a series of relief slots in the workpiece to free up cut-offs through the curve. This technique can be used for all cuts to help reduce the weight of the workpiece by removing the waste. The simplest way to do this is to make a cut in from the edge of the workpiece to the tightest point on the radius to be cut, as shown in the top photo, and then back the workpiece away from the blade.

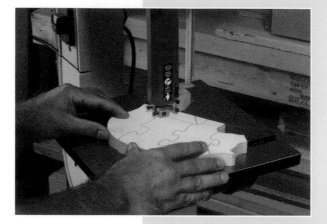

Don't skimp on relief cuts; they only take a few seconds and you'll find it's a lot easier to navigate sharp turns. Once you've made your relief cuts, go back and start cutting the curve. When you get to the tightest point of the radius, one or more sections of the workpiece should be freed, as shown in the middle photo. This extra space will make it easier to continue the cut. This is particularly useful if you discover the blade you're using is too wide for the cut and you don't have a narrower blade to install.

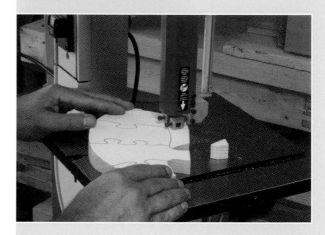

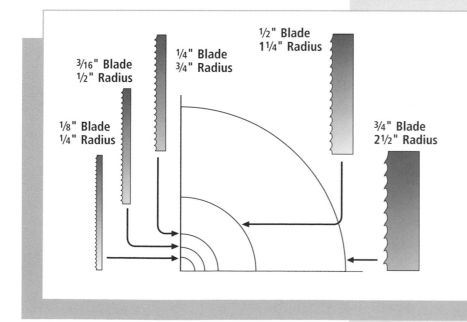

1/8" Blade
1/4" Radius

3/16" Blade
1/2" Radius

1/4" Blade
3/4" Radius

1/2" Blade
1 1/4" Radius

3/4" Blade
2 1/2" Radius

RADIUS RULES

When it comes to matching a blade to the desired radius you want to cut, the general rule of thumb is the narrower the blade, the tighter a radius it can turn. The drawing at left identifies common blade widths and the tightest radius that each can safely handle.

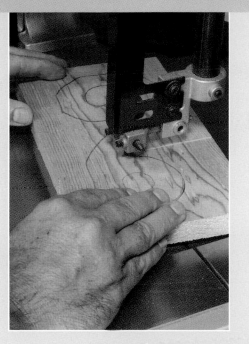

Curve-Cutting Tips

Anytime you're faced with cutting complex curves, you can make the job easier by using some of the tips described here.

Make relief cuts first

Even if you have a narrow blade on your band saw, it's a good idea to make a set of relief cuts before cutting the curve to shape as shown in the top photo. Not only do relief cuts make it easier to navigate corners, they also allow you to remove waste portions as you cut. This both lightens the workpiece and prevents sawdust from building up in the kerf.

Break up long combination cuts

The relief cuts will do a lot to break up long combination cuts. Even if you don't make relief cuts, you can still break up long curves by making a series of curved cuts. In cases like this, it's best to come into the curve at a tangent, as shown in the middle photo. This works especially well at pattern points where there's a transition from a flat to a curve, as shown here.

Rough out complex curves

Another curve-cutting tip for complex curves is to rough out the curve before cutting to the pattern line. This will also lighten the workpiece and will also make it easier to make a series of shorter relief cuts. If there are any straight portions of the pattern, cut these now to make it easier to enter the pattern where it transitions from a straight to a curved line, as shown in the bottom photo.

Angled Cuts

All band saws are capable of making angled cuts—even if their tables don't tilt; most tables tilt in one direction only to a maximum of around 45 degrees. If you want your table to tilt more, or in the opposite direction, you can build an angled sled as described at right.

Adjusting the table

The bevel indicators on most tilting tables are not very reliable. In most cases, it's best to check the angle with a protractor or adjustable triangle. If you don't have either of these, cut a scrap piece to the desired angle and use this as a visual aid to set the table angle. Once you've set the table angle and locked it in place (top photo),

you can begin cutting (middle photo). Note that when bevel-sawing you're removing more wood than if you were cutting at 90 degrees. That's because the distance between the surfaces of the wood is longer at an angle than when at 90 degrees. So slow down your feed rate to match the cutting ability of the blade.

Angled sleds

An angled sled is just a couple of scraps glued together to create an angled platform for your workpiece, as shown in the photo below right. One way to make a sled is to cut a scrap to the desired angle and then attach a thin plywood top. Alternatively, you can cut an angled scrap and fasten it directly to the underside of your workpiece with double-sided tape to tilt the workpiece to the desired angle.

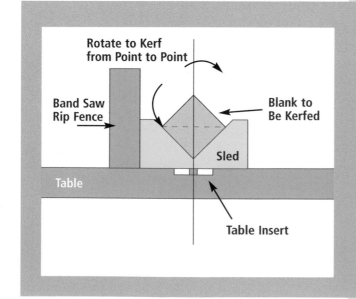

Rotate to Kerf from Point to Point

Band Saw Rip Fence

Blank to Be Kerfed

Sled

Table

Table Insert

KERFING SLED

If you're a woodturner, you know that the ends of turning blanks are kerfed to create a purchase for the lathe's drive centers. The sled shown in the drawing at left is a great way to kerf blanks—especially if you've got a lot of them to kerf at a single time. Instead of angling the table, the sled holds the blanks at the correct angle. To use the sled, position your rip fence so the blade is centered on the bottom of the V. Then simply place a blank in the sled and slide it forward to kerf the blank. Pull back, rotate the blank, and cut a second kerf if desired.

Working with Long Stock

Occasionally you'll find the need to cut long stock on the band saw. Because the tables of most saws are small, you'll need to add some kind of support to make an accurate cut. Support options include rollers stands, table extensions, and outriggers.

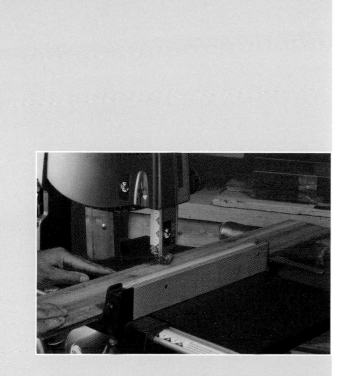

Roller stands

Manufactured and shop-made roller stands can be set up on the infeed and/or outfeed side of the saw table to support the workpiece as you make the cut.

Supports with rollers (as shown in the top photo) are common but tend to skew the workpiece to one side or another if not perfectly parallel to the back edge of the saw. Supports with curved plastic tops like the Triton multi-stand (www.triton.net.au) provide the necessary support without skewing the workpiece.

Shop-made table extensions

A simple way to add support when cutting long stock is to use a larger saw table. The shop-made table shown in the middle photo effectively doubles the working surface of the table top. Plans and detailed instructions for the table shown here can be found on pages 99–102.

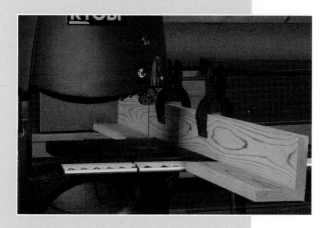

Shop-made outriggers

Another way to provide support when ripping long boards is to make a simple outrigger and attach it to your rip fence as shown in the bottom photo. The outrigger is nothing more than a long board with a pair of shorter supports underneath that are glued and screwed perpendicular to the ends to form "L's" on the infeed and outfeed sides of the saw. This simple jig does a great job of supporting most long stock.

Cutting Narrow Stock

Band saws excel at cutting narrow stock safely, as there's little chance of kickback as there is with a table saw. Also, because the opening around the blade is much smaller than the opening around the blade of a table saw, the workpiece or waste piece is much less likely to fall into the opening and jam the blade—something that's very common when cutting narrow stock on a table saw.

There's only one problem when cutting narrow stock on the band saw. If you use a standard-height rip fence, the fence will interfere with the upper guide assembly and blade guard. This situation can leave a lot of blade exposed and is unsafe. The solution to this problem is to use a low auxiliary fence designed to handle narrow cuts, as shown in the top left photo.

A low auxiliary fence consists of two scraps of wood glued or screwed together as illustrated in the drawing below. Cut the fence to match the height of your rip fence. Then place this next to your fence and slide both over until the auxiliary fence contacts the upper guide assembly. Now measure from the rip fence (not the auxiliary fence) to the blade and cut a 1/4"-thick base to match this width. Screw or glue the base piece to the auxiliary fence.

LOW FENCE FOR THIN OR NARROW STOCK

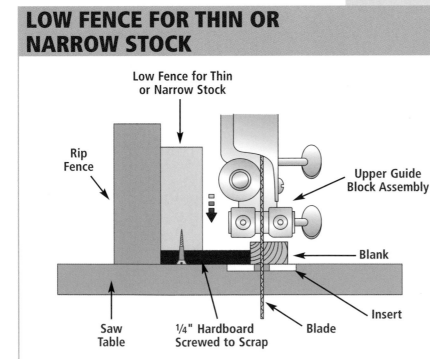

Low Fence for Thin or Narrow Stock

Rip Fence

Upper Guide Block Assembly

Blank

Insert

Blade

1/4" Hardboard Screwed to Scrap

Saw Table

Setting up the fence

To use the low auxiliary fence, clamp or screw the fence to your rip fence (our rip fence has slots in it just for situations like this—if yours doesn't, consider drilling a couple of holes in it for attaching auxiliary fences). Then simply slide the low fence over for the desired width of cut as shown in the middle photo. Make sure to switch to a push stick as you near the end of the cut.

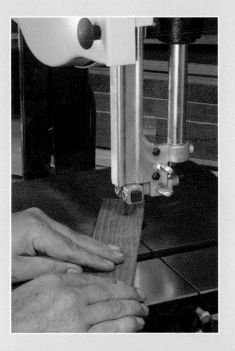

Working Safely with Small Pieces

A band saw is often the best cutting tool of choice when working with small stock for the same reasons it excels at cutting narrow stock: minimal kickback and small opening around the blade. But because a band saw blade can cut flesh as easily as wood, it's important to use one of the techniques described below to safely cut small pieces. These techniques include starting with an oversized blank, using a sled, and holding the piece with clamps.

Use oversized blanks

The first method for working with small parts may seem a bit obvious, but it's often overlooked—start with an oversized blank, as shown in the top photo. As you make your cuts, make sure to leave a "handle" or two on the small part until you're almost finished cutting. Then use the handle to guide the workpiece past the blade to separate the small part.

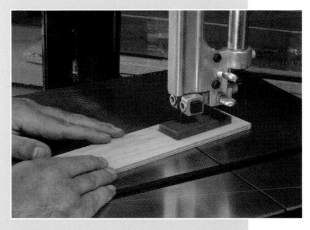

Attach to sled

Another method for cutting small parts is to attach the small part to a scrapwood "sled" or backer board as shown in the middle photo. This keeps your fingers well away from the saw blade. As with using an oversized blank, you'll need to leave a "handle" on the sled to allow you to finish cutting before separating the part as described above.

Hold with clamps

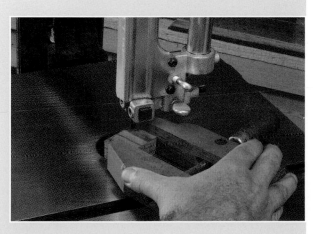

If for any reason you absolutely must work with a small part, consider holding it with a clamp as shown in the bottom photo. Small wood handscrews like the one shown here work well for this, as their square jaws can firmly grip the edges of the workpiece. Small spring clamps can also be used, as long as they grip the workpiece securely.

Cutting Round Stock

Some projects call for working with round stock. You may need to crosscut, rip, or even kerf round stock, and the band saw can easily handle each of these tasks.

Crosscuts

Since round stock will roll on a saw table, you should always cut it with some type of holding device to keep it from rotating as you cut. Holders can be made by cutting a V-notch or a groove in a scrap of wood. Then place the round stock in the holder and make your cut, as shown in the top photo.

Ripping

Ripping round stock should always be done with a holder similar to the one used to crosscut. The only difference is that you'll need to cut it to match the length of your round stock. The holder shown in the middle photo is a scrap of MDF (medium-density fiberboard) with a V-groove milled down its center.

In use, it's positioned against a rip fence and adjusted for the desired cut. Then you simply slide the holder along the fence, taking care to stop before the blade cuts the holder completely in half—this way you can use it again. It's surprisingly easy to create half-round molding this way by splitting a dowel in two.

Kerfing dowels for wedges

Some projects that call for round tenons to join parts together use wedges to lock the round tenon in a round mortise. Kerfing dowels is easily accomplished with one of the holders described above. You can cut the kerf freehand or use a fence and a stop block for added precision.

Cutting Non-Wood Materials

A band saw can tackle other materials than wood, including, metal, plastic, and composites.

Metal

Nonferrous metal like thin aluminum can be safely cut on the band saw, as long as you use a metal-cutting blade, as shown in the top photo. The general rule of thumb is that the blade should always have at least three teeth in contact with the workpiece at all times. This means thinner metal requires finer teeth. Aluminum cuts easily on the band saw but tends to load up the gullets with chips quickly. One way to prevent this is to use a blade with a coarse pitch. Alternatively, you can take light cuts and stop frequently to clear chips from the blade. This can be accomplished with the power off by pressing a brass-bristle brush up against the teeth and turning the band saw wheel by hand.

Plastic

Plastic can also be cut on band saws using a fine blade. Plastics that cut well include acrylic and sheet plastic such as Plexiglas, as shown in the middle photo. Soft plastics should be cut with a coarse blade and a slow feed rate, as they tend to gum up the blade. The last thing you want to do when cutting plastic is to stop moving the workpiece. If you do, friction will heat the blade and melt the plastic. When this happens, you'll likely fuse the kerf together and won't be able to backtrack.

Composites

A relative newcomer in the materials world is composites. Composites, like those shown in the bottom photo, are primarily used for outdoor building, including but not limited to decks, patios, and outdoor furniture. Composites are typically a hybrid of plastic mixed with wood chips or dust and are easily cut on the band saw with standard blades.

4 Advanced Band Saw Techniques

Even if you stopped with the basic techniques for using a band saw, you'd have a lot of new skills and the ability to cut wood in ways no other power tool can. When you add the advanced techniques you'll find in this chapter to your skill set, you'll be able to better shape and mill wood so you can tackle more challenging projects.

In this chapter we'll show you how to make compound cuts like those used to shape cabriole legs, how to use a simple pattern-cutting guide to easily duplicate parts, how to cut tapers, and how to resaw, including how to make your own veneer and lumber. We'll cover using a portable band saw and finish up with joinery that you can cut on the band saw, including: half-laps, tenons, mortises (yes, really), and even dovetails.

Once you've mastered basic band saw techniques, you can delve into advanced techniques like resawing. One special use of resawing is making your own lumber from logs.

Compound Cuts

When most woodworkers think of compound cuts, they think of cutting crown molding on a miter saw or making complex cuts on the table saw using a tilted blade and an angled miter gauge. But compound sawing on the band saw doesn't have to involve any angled cutting at all (you can, of course, make a standard compound cut by angling both the saw table and the miter gauge). Instead, two sets of cuts are made on adjacent sides of a workpiece to sculpt the part. The most well-known example of this is cabriole legs, as shown in the sidebar on page 65.

Double the pattern

A three-dimensional shape is easy to make on the band saw using the compound sawing technique. A pattern is applied to two adjoining sides of a blank. Then one side is cut. The waste from the first side is re-attached to the workpiece and the second side is cut to form the 3-D part. To make a compound cut on the band saw, start by cutting two patterns to fit the blank, and then attach them to the blank with spray adhesive or rubber cement. Alternatively, if you're using a template instead of a pattern, trace the template profile onto the workpiece as shown in the top photo (the pattern shown here is for the curved back slat of a chair). If the part you're making is supposed to be a true 3-D piece, take care to orient the patterns on the adjoining sides so the bottoms align and they are centered on the blank. If either of these is off, the part will come out lopsided.

Cut one profile

With the pattern attached to or marked on your blank, set up the saw to cut one of the profiles. If your blank is square, it doesn't matter much which profile you cut first. On rectangular blanks like the one shown in the middle photo, we've found that it's easiest to cut the thinner profile first. This way after the first profile has been cut and the waste pieces taped back onto the blank, the next cut will be stable since it's a wider piece (as shown in the top photo on the opposite page). If you were to cut the wide profile first and then tape the pieces back onto the blank, you'll have to cut the second profile on an edge made up of taped-together parts—this is nowhere near as stable as a blank that's laid flat on the saw top.

Attach the waste

Once you've cut the first side, attach the waste pieces or cutoffs from the first cut back onto the blank as shown in the bottom photo. Masking tape or duct tape works best for this. There are two reasons you need to attach the waste pieces to the blank: The second side pattern is attached to the waste pieces and you'll need these lines to show you where to make the second cut, and also, without these pieces, the workpiece won't lie flat on the table.

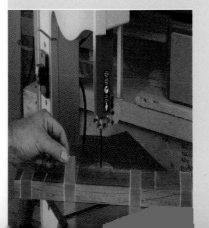

Cut the second face

When you've got the waste pieces attached to your blank, take a moment and use a pen or pencil to connect any pattern lines obscured by the tape. Then go ahead and make the cuts on the second side, as shown in the top photo. After removing all of the waste pieces, you'll be left with your 3-D part. We used this technique to create the sculpted letter opener shown on pages 172–174. We also created the cabriole legs for the stool featured on pages 184–189, as described in the sidebar below.

MAKING A CABRIOLE LEG

Cabriole legs are those delightfully S-shaped legs found on Queen Anne furniture and other period pieces. The legs may be smoothed gracefully or embellished with light relief carving on the "knees"—typically a leaf pattern, or heavy sculpted carving at the foot of the leg. The ball-and-claw foot pattern was extremely popular for a while. Antiques collectors and aficionados can even tell you when and sometimes who made a piece just by looking at the foot of a cabriole leg. The type, shape, and number of the claws, for example, are all clues they can use to help identify the maker.

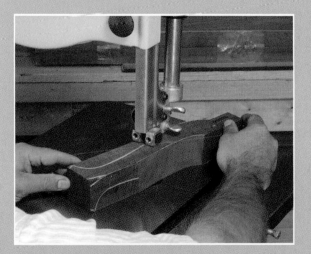

First cut one profile. As with any compound sawing task, a cabriole leg is made by tracing a pattern onto two adjacent sides of a blank. Note that since we were working with walnut, we used a white pencil to trace around the template. Adjust the saw as needed and then cut the first profile, taking care to save the waste pieces.

Then cut the second. Before you can cut the second profile, you'll need to tape the waste pieces back onto the blank so the blank will lie flat and the pattern will be visible. Cut the second profile and remove the waste pieces to expose the rough leg. Now you'll need to smooth and shape the leg as described on pages 188–189.

Pattern Cutting

Although most woodworkers don't think of a band saw as a duplicating machine, it can be with the addition of a simple shop-made pattern-cutting fence. The pattern-cutting fence is a simple device that clamps to the saw table and "hugs" the blade; see the sidebar on the opposite page.

PATTERN-CUTTING ACTION

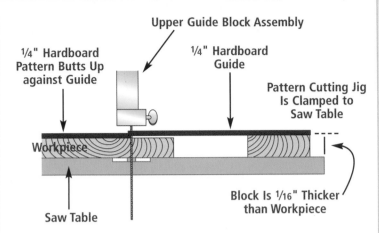

PATTERN-CUTTING ACTION

Upper Guide Block Assembly

¼" Hardboard Pattern Butts Up against Guide

¼" Hardboard Guide

Pattern Cutting Jig Is Clamped to Saw Table

Workpiece

Saw Table

Block Is ¹/₁₆" Thicker than Workpiece

Pattern-cutting action

To use the fence, you first attach a template of the piece you want to duplicate to a blank. Then you simply butt the template up against the business end of the fence and make your cut, keeping the edge of the template in constant contact with the tip of the fence. Any excess waste on the blank passes under the guide and is trimmed off to match the template, as illustrated in the top drawing. When you've cut around the entire perimeter of the template, the blank will be an exact duplicate. This is particularly useful when you need to duplicate irregular-shaped parts for a project.

Set up the pattern-cutting fence

To set up the pattern-cutting fence, position the fence on the saw table so it's in line with the blade, as shown in the middle photo. Then clamp the fence securely to the saw table.

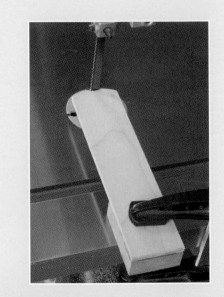

Attach a pattern to the blank

Once the fence is set up, you can ready the blank. One way to attach the template to the blank is with double-sided tape, as shown in the bottom photo. It's always a good idea to use a couple of strips the full length of the template to ensure a good grip. This technique is commonly used in production environments, except they don't temporarily tape the template to a blank—instead they use a vacuum clamp. The template is placed onto a blank, the vacuum clamp is engaged, and the part is cut—very quick and efficient.

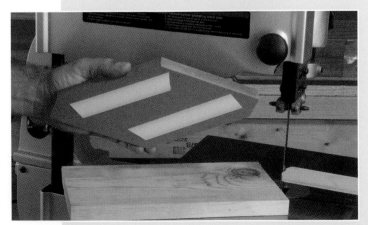

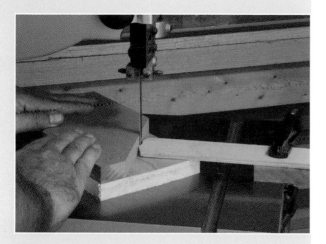

Creating a duplicate part

With the template attached to your blank, turn on the saw and simply push the blank into the blade until the template makes contact with the tip of the guide. Then just slide the blank/template forward, keeping the template in constant contact with the tip of the guide. Repeat for the entire perimeter of the template. When complete, turn off the saw and remove the template from the blank. If your double-sided tape is stubborn about releasing its grip, drizzle a few drops of lacquer thinner onto the joint. The lacquer thinner will dissolve the glue bond of the tape, and the template will release from the blank.

PATTERN-CUTTING FENCE

The pattern-cutting fence is just a pair of scraps glued or screwed together. The base of the jig should be at least 1/16" thicker than the blank you want to cut so that the blank can fit easily under the 1/4" hardboard guide that sits on top of the base, as illustrated in the drawing.

Because the fence clamps to your saw table, you'll want to measure from the edge of the saw table to the blade and cut the guide to match this measurement. The base need only be a couple inches long. Cut both pieces to a width of around 2" and glue them together. Cut or sand a gradual curve on the end of the guide, and then carefully mark and cut a notch to fit around the blade. Try to cut this only as wide as the blade you'll be using. This will create the maximum rub surface for the template.

FENCE ANATOMY

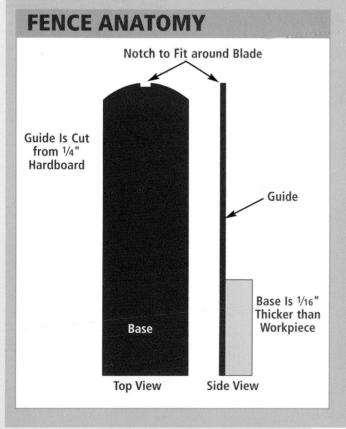

Notch to Fit around Blade

Guide Is Cut from 1/4" Hardboard

Guide

Base Is 1/16" Thicker than Workpiece

Base

Top View   Side View

■ COPYING CURVES

A pattern-cutting fence does a good job of creating duplicate parts, but did you know that you can copy curves on a band saw without a pattern-cutting fence? You can. All it takes is a rub block or a single-point resaw fence. (See pages 118–119 for directions on how to make a single-point resaw fence.) Alternatively, if you made the band saw table and fence shown on pages 99–107, there's a single-point resaw attachment you can make for it as described on pages 108–109 and shown here. This technique is particularly useful for making thin curved slats like you'd install in the back of a chair, bench, or rocker.

Curved slats. Here's how it works. Start by laying out the desired curve on a wide blank. The wider the blank, the more parts you can duplicate. Then cut one side of the curve as shown in the top photo. If you're making a lot of parts and have multiple blanks, lay out and cut the first curve on each blank.

Now you can set up your rub block. Position the block or resaw fence or attachment so that it is aligned with the blade (as shown in the photo at right) and is the desired distance away from the blade. This distance will determine the width of the duplicated parts. For example, if you set the rub block ¾" away from the blade, your parts will all come out ¾" wide.

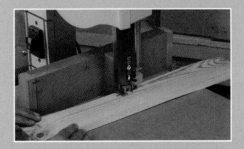

Turn on the saw and butt the curved profile of the blank against the rub block. Slide the blank forward, keeping the curved edge of the blank as perpendicular to the rub block as possible, as shown in the above photo at right. Continue pushing the blank forward until the first part has been cut. Then repeat this procedure for as many parts as you can get out of the blank.

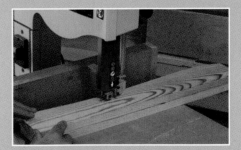

Stacked cuts. If you really need to bang out a lot of duplicate curved parts, you can combine this technique with stacking—that is, just fasten together a couple of blanks at a time with double-sided tape. Lay out and cut the first curve as shown in the second photo from the bottom. Then position your rub block and cut the parts to shape as shown in the bottom photo.

Cutting Tapers

Tapers can be cut on the band saw two ways: free-hand and with a taper jig. For best results, we recommend that you use a shop-made taper jig like the one described here. With a taper jig for the band saw you can cut tapers on parts such as table legs, bench legs, and stool legs. A good taper jig should also allow you to taper just about any part for any use. To be useful, a taper jig should be easily adjustable to cut a wide range of taper angles, and it should also be adjustable to handle a variety of workpiece sizes. The shop-made taper jig illustrated in the top drawing does both. Plus it features a taper block with an index pin that holds both ends of the part to be tapered securely in place as the workpiece passes by the saw blade.

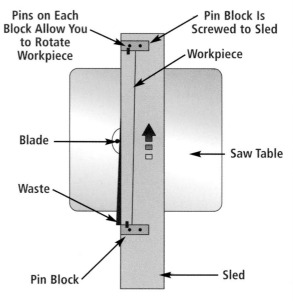

TAPER-CUTTING JIG

Pins on Each Block Allow You to Rotate Workpiece

Pin Block Is Screwed to Sled

Workpiece

Blade

Saw Table

Waste

Pin Block

Sled

Build the taper jig

The taper jig illustrated in the top drawing consists of a sled and a pair of blocks that hold each end of the blank to be tapered. An index pin or dowel passes through both blocks into holes drilled into the ends of the blank. The amount of taper is adjusted by positioning the blocks on the sled. These are simply screwed to the sled where needed. When you need to cut a different taper, just unscrew one or both blocks and reposition them as desired. The big advantage of using pins to support the blank is that you can safely and accurately taper all four sides of the blank if desired.

Attach the blank

To use the taper jig, start by drilling a centered hole on the end of each blank. For the jig shown here, we used 1/4" dowels for the pins and so drilled 1/4"-diameter, 3/8"-deep holes. Once you've drilled the holes, attach

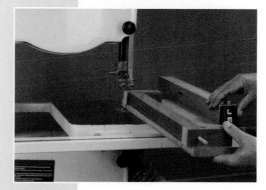

the blank to the taper blocks via the dowel pins as shown in the middle photo. Then position the blank and blocks on the sled so the bottom of the blank extends out past the edge of the blank the desired taper. Adjust the position of the top block to define the starting point of the taper and then screw both blocks to the sled.

Adjust the rip fence

With the blank attached to the sled, butt the sled up against your rip fence and slide it over so the edge of the base just contacts the blade, and lock the fence in place as shown in the bottom photo.

Cut the first taper

Lower the upper guide assembly of the saw until it's about 1/8" above the blank, and turn on the saw. To cut the first taper, simply push the sled forward, keeping it firmly butted up against the rip fence as shown in the top photo. Push the sled completely past the blade, turn the saw off, and when the blade has come to a complete stop, pull the sled back into its starting position.

Rotate blank and cut the next taper

To cut another taper, pull the index pins out and rotate the blank to expose the next side you want to taper. Replace the pins and repeat the cutting procedure described above to taper the second side, as shown in the middle photo.

Repeat for remaining sides if desired

If you'd like, taper one or both of the remaining sides of the blank as shown in the bottom photo. Note that even though there's a gap between the blank and the sled, the blank is firmly supported by the pins in the taper blocks.

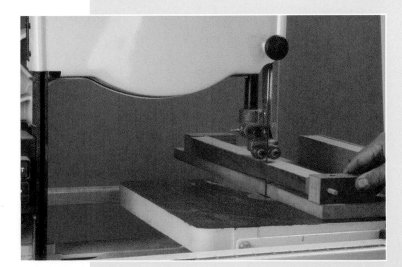

■ CLEANING UP TAPERS

There's only one real disadvantage to cutting tapers on the band saw—the surfaces of the taper will have saw marks from the blade. This really isn't a big deal because there are a number of quick and easy ways to remove these marks to leave a smooth surface. These include smoothing surfaces with a power jointer and doing so by hand with a hand plane or cabinet scraper.

Jointer. A jointer can make quick work of cleaning up the surfaces of a leg tapered on the band saw. Often all that's required is a single pass. Set your jointer for a fine cut (around 1/16") and place the tapered part on the bed of the jointer so that the taper is flat on the bed, as shown in the top photo. Then use a push block to advance the part over the rotating jointer knives. Use a slow feed rate to create as smooth a surface as possible. Rotate the part and joint additional surfaces as needed.

Hand plane. If you're not in a hurry (or if you don't have a jointer), you can clean up tapered surfaces easily with a hand plane. Clamp the blank to your bench as shown in the middle photo and set your hand plane for a fine shaving. Take care to plane with the grain. With a sharp blade, you can often clean up a surface with just a stroke or two with the plane—and this is a lot more satisfying (and quieter) than using a jointer.

Hand scraper. A hand scraper looks like a 3 × 5 index card made of metal. This simple tool is surprisingly effective at removing saw mark ridges. The magic of a hand scraper is a burr that's rolled onto the edge with a burnisher. Just like a hand plane, skewing a scraper produces more of a shearing cut and will likely produce nicer shavings, as shown in the bottom photo. Keep in mind that using a hand scraper can be fatiguing, as you normally bow the scraper as you cut and need to hold it at a specific angle for it to cut well. One way around this is to use a cabinet scraper. These handy tools basically hold a scraper blade at the correct angle while bowing it at the same time. These are much easier on the hands when you've got a lot of scraping to do.

Resawing

Resawing is a technique where you cut through the thickness of a workpiece to create thinner stock. The band saw is the perfect tool for the job. Yes, you can resaw with a table saw; but you're limited to the maximum cut of the saw, and the kerf created by a table saw blade wastes a lot of good wood. A typical stationary band saw can resaw wood up to around 6" in width—and up to 12" in width by adding a height attachment as described on page 13. Resawing is simple enough if you follow the setup instructions and techniques described here. What can be a challenge is dealing with the wood once it's been cut.

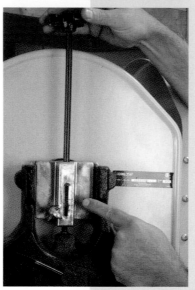

What many woodworkers aren't aware of is that wood that's been kiln-dried has a different moisture level on the surface of the wood compared to its core. Additionally, there are tensions within the wood that are created in the drying and conditioning processes. When you resaw a board, two things happen: You expose higher-moisture-content wood to air, and you release some of the tensions within the wood. In effect, you end up with a thinner piece of wood that has a higher moisture content on one face versus the other face—the perfect recipe for wood movement.

This means you should always expect a resawn board to warp or twist a bit. To remove the warp, you'll need to plane or joint the face and edges true—that's why you should always resaw boards 1/8" to 1/4" thicker than your desired finished thickness. Note that some boards have so much internal tension that they'll bow or cup as they're being cut. There really isn't anything you can do about this except to try another board.

Since you remove a lot of wood when resawing, there are a few ways to make this easier on the saw. These include using the correct blade, increasing the tension, and using dust collection.

Install the correct blade

If you're planning on resawing any wood over 2" in width, you should definitely install a resaw blade. In most cases, this is the widest blade that your saw will accept. The typical 14" stationary saw will take up to a 3/4"-wide blade. The blade we use for resawing is called the Resaw King and is manufactured by Laguna Tools (www.lagunatools.com) and has carbide tips that really plow through the wood, as shown in the top photo.

Increase tension

With the correct blade installed, you'll want to tension it properly. The most common problem when resawing—bowing—is caused by insufficient tension. The blade deflects under the cutting pressure and results in a barrel cut (see page 169 for an example of this). For most resawing, it's best to increase the tension at least one blade width greater than the blade you're using. So if you've installed a 1/2"-wide blade, tension it at 3/4", as shown in the middle photo.

Dust collection

Finally, make sure to hook up some form of dust collection to your saw to deal with the copious amount of dust that resawing will produce, as shown in the bottom photo.

■ RESAWING FENCE OPTIONS

One of the challenges with resawing is that the workpiece is cut one its edge. With wood less than 1" in thickness, this can be very unstable. That's why it's so important to support the workpiece as much as possible. There are two common ways to support the workpiece: with a tall fence, or with a single-point contact fence. (Additionally, a tall featherboard can be used to press the workpiece into the fence, as described on page 75.) Both fences can tackle the problem of blade "lead" or "drift" as described on page 74.

Tall fence. One method to support a workpiece for resawing is to build a sturdy fence like the one shown in the photo at left and illustrated in the top drawing. The fence is just two pieces of MDF or plywood screwed together at a right angle, with triangular support blocks added to provide rigidity and ensure a 90-degree cut. (Note: Cutting a notch near the saw's guide assembly lets you lower the assembly when resawing short workpieces.) The fence is then clamped to your saw table to create the desired cut.

Single-contact point fence. A second support option favored by many woodworkers is a single-point fence like the one shown in the photo at left and illustrated in the bottom drawing. The advantage this fence has over a full-length fence is that it allows you to compensate for variations within the wood itself as you make the cut. Basically you clamp the fence to your saw table so the point of the fence is set away from the blade the desired distance. In use, butt one face of the workpiece against the tip of the fence and feed it into the blade, adjusting the angle of the feed as desired to cut a uniformly thick piece.

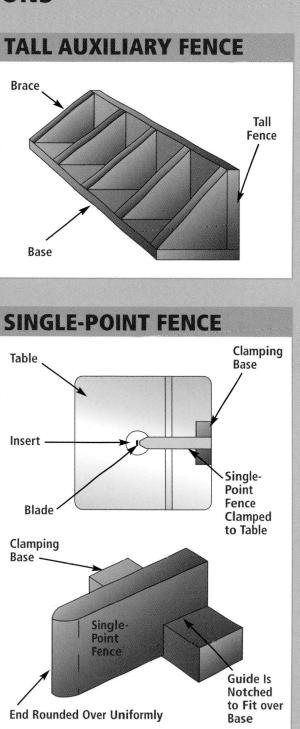

TALL AUXILIARY FENCE

Brace

Tall Fence

Base

SINGLE-POINT FENCE

Table

Clamping Base

Insert

Blade

Single-Point Fence Clamped to Table

Clamping Base

Single-Point Fence

End Rounded Over Uniformly

Guide Is Notched to Fit over Base

Mark the edge of the workpiece

A common problem that occurs when resawing is "drift." Drift is a blade's natural tendency to pull a workpiece in one direction when cutting. It's caused by a blade that has an uneven set—that is, the set (or amount each tooth is bent away from the blade) is not the same on both sides. To compensate for drift, it's necessary to shift the fence to match the drift. To identify the amount and angle of drift on a blade, start by marking a line down the length of a scrap of wood along its edge, as shown in the top photo.

Check for drift

Now adjust the upper guide assembly for a safe cut and turn on the saw. Feed the scrap into the blade, taking care to cut along the marked line. Odds are that you'll have to angle the scrap one way or another to accomplish this; don't fight this—let the blade cut its own way, as shown in the middle photo. When you've reached about the midway point, stop and turn off the saw, holding the scrap to prevent it from moving. The angle of the scrap is the angle of the blade's drift, and your fence needs to match this if you don't want to fight the blade. It's important to remember that this angle relates only to the current blade on the band saw; if you change blades, you'll need to recheck for drift—it'll almost certainly be different.

Adjust the fence as needed

There are a couple of ways to transfer this angle to your fence. If you have a rip fence that is adjustable, simply loosen the appropriate bolts to friction-tight and butt the fence up against the scrap until the angles match before retightening the bolts. If you're using a clamp-on fence, lightly trace the angle of the scrap onto your saw top with a pencil. Then when you set up your fence, just make sure it's parallel to this line, as shown in the bottom photo.

Adding featherboards

In addition to using a fence, the next best thing you can do to support a workpiece when resawing is to use a featherboard. A standard featherboard won't do much for you here except press the base of the workpiece into the fence. What you need is a vertical featherboard like the one shown in the top photo. This type of featherboard applies pressure along the full width of a workpiece to help ensure a uniform cut. Step-by-step plans and instructions for the shop-made featherboard shown here can be found on pages 94–95.

Use a slow feed rate

With everything set up, you can turn on the saw (and dust collection) and then guide the workpiece into the blade as shown in the middle photo. Use steady, even pressure here. Don't force the cut—let the blade do the work. Remember, you're removing a lot of material here—it's slow going, even with a sharp blade. If you notice that the workpiece is pulling away from the fence, stop, recheck drift, and re-adjust the fence position to eliminate this.

Use a push stick at end of cut

As you complete the cut, use a push block to safely push the workpiece past the saw blade, as shown in the bottom photo. Unfortunately, it's not until the blade exits the workpiece that you'll find out whether you've got a bowing or "barreling" problem. If you do, you'll need to increase the blade tension and try again. After you've resawn a board, it's a good idea to "sticker" the pieces as described on page 127 to allow air to circulate evenly around the cut faces. Let the boards sit for a couple of days if possible, or overnight at minimum, before machining them.

■ MAKING YOUR OWN VENEER

Cutting your own veneer has a number of advantages. It saves money, of course. And by using the same wood as the rest of your project, the veneer you cut will match perfectly. What's more, you can custom-cut the veneer to any thickness you want. All it takes is a band saw with a sharp blade, a couple of shop-made jigs, and some patience.

Adjust the fence. To cut veneer on a band saw, you'll need a tall fence to support the wood during the cut. We recommend making a sturdy fence like the one shown in the middle photo and described on page 73. You'll need to check and adjust for drift (as described on page 74) before clamping the fence in its final position to create the desired thickness of veneer.

Add a featherboard. Another simple jig that helps ensure accuracy is a featherboard that presses the workpiece firmly against the fence, as shown in the middle photo and described on page 74 and detailed on pages 94–95. Make sure to position the featherboard so it exerts pressure on the workpiece approximately ¼" in front of the blade. If you place it at or behind the blade, it'll just cause the veneer to bind against the blade and you'll end up with a ragged and/or burned surface.

Make the cut. There are a couple of band saw requirements that are critical for successfully cutting veneer. The blade must be the right type and it must be sharp. We use a ¾"-wide, 4-tooth-per-inch blade because it's designed for resawing. The gullets on this type of blade are deeper, which allows for better waste removal and cooler cuts.

The saw must also be adjusted properly. Make sure the guide blocks and thrust bearings are in the correct position. Increase the blade tension to at least the next blade width. Then lower the blade guard as close to the workpiece as possible and turn on the saw and guide the workpiece into the blade as shown in the bottom photo. Use steady, even pressure. Don't force the cut—let the blade do the work. Remember, you're removing a lot of material here—it's slow going. As you complete the cut, use a push block to safely push the workpiece past the saw blade.

One of the best things about cutting your own veneer is that you can cut it to any thickness and orient the grain any way you want. The following grain patterns also apply to cutting your own lumber, as described on page 78.

There are three main ways to cut a log into veneer or lumber: a through-and-through or "flitch" cut, quarter- or rift-sawing, and plain-sawing or "sawing for grade," as illustrated in the drawing at right. The difference among the three is how the growth rings of the log are oriented to the cut.

When a log is cut through and through, the lumber is cut tangentially to the growth rings. With quartersawing, the log is divided into quarters or thirds and then each section is cut radially to the growth rings. If a log is sawn for grade, it's rotated as it's cut to yield the best lumber; this produces flatsawn lumber along with rift- and quartersawn.

Plainsawn. A plain- or flat-sawn board is the most common type of lumber, as this cutting method produces the best yield from a log. The grain on the face of the board will often swirl in many directions. When a wild-grained piece of wood like this is stained, the softer, more porous earlywood will soak up more stain and be darker than the harder, less porous latewood. The resulting pattern is often referred to as "landscape figure." Flatsawn lumber tends to move a lot with changes in humidity—it often cups and warps.

Riftsawn. Riftsawn lumber generally has clearer, straighter grain than plain-sawn lumber. You'll often find riftsawn lumber in the same stack as plainsawn. In some cases, you may even see both types of wood in a single board—this is what sawyers call a "bastard" cut. The face grain will have wilder gain on one side and straighter, more even grain on the other. Generally, you should avoid boards like this, as the two sides will react differently to changes in humidity. True riftsawn lumber is more stable than plainsawn and tends to warp less.

Quartersawn. Of all the cutting methods, quartersawing produces boards that are the most stable. Quartersawn lumber shows the straightest grain and in some species will exhibit ray fleck. Ray fleck is common in quartersawn white oak, red oak, sycamore, and cherry. But beauty like this exacts a price. Quarter-sawing is the most wasteful way to cut up a log, it's time-consuming, it's expensive, and you need a much larger log to produce reasonably wide boards.

VARIOUS CUTS

Through-and-Through
or
Flitch Cut

Quarter- and Riftsawn

Plainsawn

Making Your Own Lumber

Making your own lumber is easy with a band saw. There are only a couple of special rules. First, you should always fasten the lumber to be cut to some form of sled so that it won't wobble during a cut. Second, since most wood you'll be cutting will be green and therefore wet, you must take care to clean and dry your saw after cutting lumber to size.

Attach wood to sled

A simple sled does two things for you. It prevents the log or flitch from rocking or wobbling during a cut due to its uneven surfaces, and it also provides an accurate straight edge to use as a reference against the rip fence to create uniformly thick boards. Start by splitting your log (or cutting it with a chainsaw) as needed until you have a piece that your saw can handle—for most 14" band saws, this means a blank around 5" thick. Then cut a scrap of plywood or MDF (as shown here) slightly wider than your blank and at least as long. Drill a couple of countersunk pilot holes near the rip fence edge in the bottom of the sled, and screw your blank to it as shown in the top right photo. Coarse-thread screws work best in green wood.

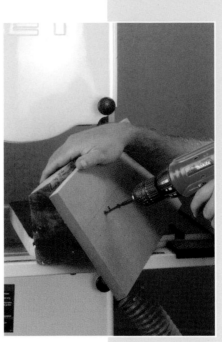

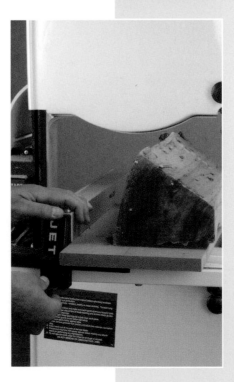

Adjust for desired thickness

To set up for a cut, make sure to have the widest blade on your saw that it can handle and increase the tension one blade width greater than the width of the blade you're using. Position the sled and blank on the saw top and slide the rip fence for the first cut (bottom left photo). You're looking to create a full-width flat surface, so adjust the fence accordingly.

Cut the boards

Turn on the saw and make your first cut using s slow, steady feed rate. When complete, reposition the rip fence for the desired thickness and cut your first board (bottom right photo). Repeat until you've cut up to the mounting screws holding the blank in place and stop. Sticker the boards as shown on page 127. The only disadvantage to this technique is that your sled will get cut up along with the lumber. To get around this, consider building the sliding lumber sled described on pages 122–127.

Using a Portable Band Saw

A portable band saw makes quick work of many tough sawing jobs. Anyone that's ever worked up a sweat cutting a piece of metal with a hacksaw will appreciate how fast and effortlessly a portable band saw can do the job. Although they look a bit intimidating, a portable band saw is easy to use and relatively safe as long as you follow some basic safety rules. And unlike a stationary band saw, where you bring the work to the blade, on a portable band saw you present the blade to the workpiece. This means you've got both hands on the saw and the likelihood of a cut finger is greatly reduced.

Clamp the workpiece securely

The number one rule in using a portable band saw is to securely clamp the workpiece to a bench, sawhorse, or other stable work surface, as shown in the top photo. If you have a machinist's vise handy, this is the best tool for the job. For long stock, take the time to clamp the workpiece at both ends (as shown here) to prevent the workpiece from pivoting as it's being cut. You also need to know how to orient the workpiece to the saw when you clamp it to the work surface, as illustrated in the drawing on page 80.

Proper stance

The proper stance is also important. Since portable bands saws are a bit bulky and can be heavy, you'll want to maintain an open stance with your knees bent slightly to distribute the weight of the saw. One hand will grip the handle and power switch; the other hand grips the knob or handle at the top of the saw, as shown in the photo at right.

FINDING THE CORRECT SPEED

If your portable band saw has more than one speed or is a variable-speed unit, you'll need to select the proper speed or speed range before making a cut. Many portable band saws with variable speeds allow you to vary the speed as the saw is running.

• Use higher speeds when cutting: copper, brass, bronze, aluminum, cast iron, angle iron, and mild steel.

• Use lower speeds if you're cutting: plastic pipe, tougher steels, chrome steel, tungsten steel, stainless steel, and other tough-to-cut materials.

Note that lower speeds are best for cutting plastic, as the higher speeds tend to melt plastic and fuse the kerf together behind the blade.

Make the cut

Before you make the cut, it's a good idea to check the oil level in the gear chamber; consult your owner's manual for specifics. Add lubricant as needed. Then gently lower the saw onto the workpiece so that the material guide comes into contact with the workpiece, as shown in the top photo, before turning on the saw. To avoid kickback and other potentially dangerous situations (like a broken blade or workpiece), make sure to lower the blade into the workpiece as illustrated in the drawing below.

Cutting action

As you continue to cut, take care to hold the saw so you don't twist the blade. Twisting or cocking the blade will force the blade to wander and will also dramatically shorten its life. Don't use any downward pressure; the weight of the saw is all that's required to make the cut. If you apply downward pressure, you'll only slow the saw down. Be careful as you near the end of the cut to avoid the cutoff, which can be quite hot from the cutting friction. At the end of the cut, make sure to have a firm grip on the saw; don't allow it to bang into the workpiece.

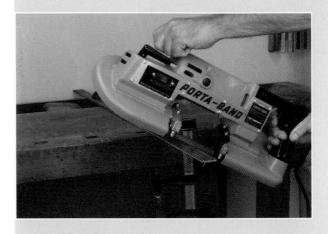

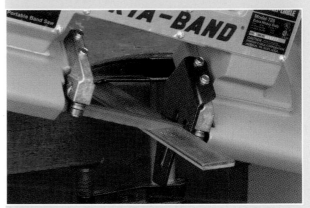

RECOMMENDED CUTTING POSITIONS

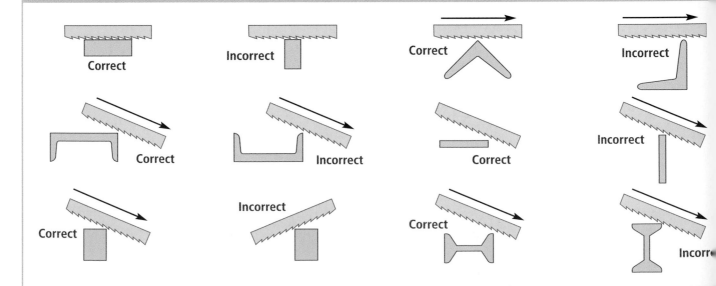

Joinery: Half-Laps

Whenever two parts are lapped over one another, a lap joint is formed. In furniture construction, both ends of the pieces are typically notched so the surfaces end up flush with one another—this joint is technically called a half-lap (as illustrated in the drawing below) and does an excellent job of resisting lateral movement. Making a lap joint on a band saw is simple: one shoulder cut and one cheek cut per piece. The challenge is getting the two halves the correct thickness so the faces end up flush.

Define the cheek

To cut a lap joint (a half-lap joint is shown here), start by setting the rip fence to define the width or cheek of the half-lap. In most cases you want to split the workpiece exactly in two. Use a metal rule to roughly position the rip fence as shown in the top photo. Then make test cuts on both ends of a scrap, Cut the piece in half and butt the cut ends together, taking care to reverse one piece so the ends are aligned as if they are to be joined. If the fence is set correctly, the cut lines will align perfectly. Adjust the fence if necessary and retest. Once the fence is set up, add a stop to define the shoulder. In most cases, this block should stop the cut at a point equal to the width of the workpiece. Use a same-width scrap to position the stop and make test cuts; adjust as needed.

Cut the cheek

Now you're ready to cut the cheeks of the half-lap joints. Turn on the saw and butt one face of a workpiece up against the rip fence. Slide the workpiece forward gently into the blade until it runs into the stop, as shown in the middle photo. Then back the workpiece off the blade; repeat this procedure for all parts to be joined with half-laps.

Cut the shoulder

The shoulder can now be cut to free the waste piece. This is easily done with the aid of a miter gauge, as shown in the bottom photo. For added precision, you can use the rip fence to define the length of the cheek; just make sure to clamp a short scrap block to the fence and butt the workpiece up against the block before sliding the workpiece forward. This way the waste piece can't be trapped between the rip fence and the blade, as it would if you only used the rip fence as the stop.

ANATOMY OF A HALF-LAP

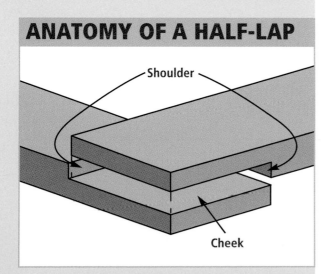

Shoulder

Cheek

Joinery: Tenons

It's well known that the mortise-and-tenon is one of the strongest joints in furniture construction. That's why it's used almost exclusively for joining together high-stress or high-load parts, such as the sides of a chair or bench. A mortise-and-tenon joint has two parts: a hole (usually square), called a mortise, made in one part (see pages 84–85 for easy-to-make mortises on the band saw), and a tenon cut on the end of the mating part. Tenons are cut by removing wood on all four sides at the end of the part, creating shoulders, as illustrated in the top drawing. Tenons are easily cut on the band saw with the aid of rip fence and a stop block. The tenon fits into the mortise and can be glued in place or held with dowels, fasteners, or even a wedge. The best way to get a mortise-and-tenon to fit together is to cut the mortise first, then cut the tenon to fit. That's because it's much easier to re-size a tenon than it is to re-cut a mortise.

Define width of the tenon

To cut a tenon on the band saw, start by adjusting your rip fence to determine the width of the tenon. You'll make a cheek cut on each face of the workpiece to do this; the waste will be removed when you make the shoulder cuts. Use a metal rule to roughly posi-

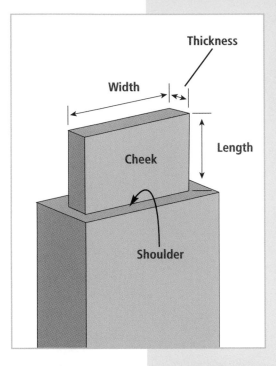

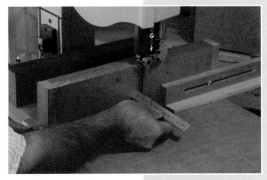

tion the rip fence as shown in the top photo. Then make test cuts on similar-thickness scraps and adjust as needed until the desired tenon width is achieved.

Define the tenon length

With the fence set correctly, the next step is to add a stop block to the fence to define the length of the tenon. Use a metal rule to position the stop, as shown in the middle photo. (We used the built-in stop of the shop-made fence shown on pages 103–107.) Make a test cut and adjust the stop as needed to get the correct tenon length.

Cut one cheek

Now you can turn on the saw and cut the first cheek. Butt the workpiece firmly against the rip fence and slide it forward into the blade until it touches the stop as shown in the bottom photo. Turn off the saw and back the workpiece off the blade.

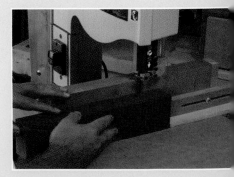

Flip and cut the other cheek

Turn the saw back on and flip the workpiece over so the opposite face is against the rip fence. Now cut the second cheek as shown in the top photo. Note that it's a good idea to either cut a small chamfer on the end of the stop block for sawdust relief or make sure to blow out any sawdust trapped between the end of the workpiece and the front of the stop after every cut. If you don't, you'll end up with different-length tenons.

Make end cuts if desired

Depending on the type of tenon you're cutting, you may or may not want to make a set of end cuts to define a tenon that's narrower than the width of the workpiece as shown in the middle photo. On many parts, this cut is the same as the cheek cuts. If not, you'll need to readjust the fence position.

Make the shoulder cuts

Finally, you can cut away the waste to expose the tenon by making a series of shoulder cuts with the aid of a miter gauge. To prevent the waste from being trapped between the rip fence and the saw blade, we replaced the rip fence with a shorter version as shown here. In use, you simply slide the workpiece over until it butts up against the short fence and then slide the workpiece forward until the waste is freed.

Joinery: Faux Mortises

The other half of a mortise-and-tenon joint—the mortise—is not something you can cut normally on a band saw: The mortise is a hole or cavity cut into the edge or face of a workpiece. Mortises come in two basic types: stopped and through. A stopped mortise does not go all the way through the workpiece; a through mortise does, as illustrated in the top drawing. Both can be cut by hand or more commonly with a router and mortising jig. There is, though, a neat way to cut a through mortise on the band saw: Don't cut a mortise. Instead, cut a pair of matching wide notches on the inside faces of two pieces and glue these together to create a "faux" through mortise. For this technique to work, the parts need to be of identical thickness, and care must be taken during glue-up.

Define one-half of mortise

To cut a faux through mortise, start by positioning a long stop block behind the blade to serve as a stop, as shown in the middle photo. This block will limit the cut to define the depth of each half-mortise. Use a metal rule to roughly position the stop block, and then make a couple of test cuts on scraps. Readjust the stop block as needed until the desired depth is achieved. Note that this is one-half of the finished mortise width.

Cut the shoulders

With the stop block set up correctly, use a miter gauge to slide the workpiece gently into the blade at each shoulder location until the workpiece butts up against the stop block, as shown in the bottom

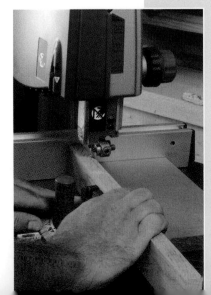

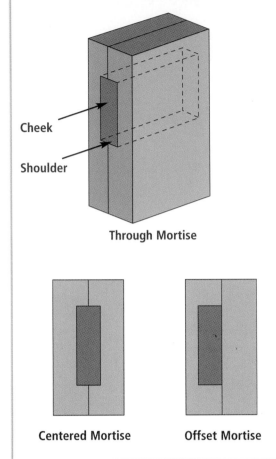

FAUX MORTISE ANATOMY

Cheek

Shoulder

Through Mortise

Centered Mortise   **Offset Mortise**

photo. Shift the workpiece as needed to cut the second shoulder. For added precision, you can use the rip fence (as shown here) as a stop to define the position of a shoulder; just note that you'll have to reposition to cut the second one. Make sure to cut all of the shoulders on all your parts before shifting the fence to cut the second shoulder.

Remove the waste: Step 1

Once the shoulders have been defined, you can remove the waste between the shoulder cuts. It's best to strike a line between the two shoulder cuts to identify the waste. Holding the workpiece on edge as shown in the top photo, cut into the waste area at around the midpoint and cut down until you meet the cut defining the shoulder. Although it'd be nice to use the rip fence as a stop to define this cut, there's no safe way to do this.

Remove the waste: Step 2

After you've cut into one corner, flip the workpiece end-for-end and start the cut in the corner you just made in the step above. Slide the workpiece forward, keeping on the waste side of the marked line, to remove the rest of the waste as shown in the middle photo. To clean up the mortise, you can reinstall the long stop in the same location that you used to define the shoulders and slide the workpiece from side to side over the spinning blade. This will effectively clean up any waste, leaving a uniform flat face of the half-mortise.

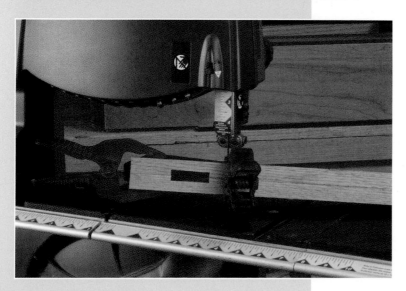

Glue up the two halves

Now you can glue up pairs of notched parts to form the faux mortises, as shown in the bottom photo. One way to ensure that the halves align is to insert a scrap tenon "key" into the mortise during assembly. The only problem is that it's easy to glue the key in place; to prevent this, apply a couple of coats of varnish to the "key" and let it dry before using it.

Joinery: Dovetails

The dovetail joint is viewed by many woodworkers as the ultimate way to join wood together. The joint is both attractive and incredibly strong. The joint gets its name from the tail half of the joint that resembles the shape of a dove's tail, as illustrated in the top drawing. The other half of the joint is the pins, which fit into the openings (or sockets) between the tails. The dovetail joints we'll be discussing here are full dovetails, as the joint is made through the full thickness of the stock. Dovetails that are formed partway through the thickness of the stock (half-blind dovetails) are best done by hand or with the aid of a router and a dovetail jig.

Cutting precise through dovetails by hand requires a steady hand, a keen eye, and razor-sharp tools—not to mention considerable practice. But much of this work can be done quickly—and accurately—on the band saw. We generally cut the tails first, and then the pins to fit. Which you cut first is really a matter of personal preference.

Define depth of tails and pins
To begin work on your dovetails, you'll need to first mark both the tail and the pin pieces to define the depth or width of the dovetails. With through dovetails, this depth or width is equal to the thickness of your stock. The quickest way to mark all your stock is to use a marking gauge or a cutting gauge, as shown in the middle photo.

Set up the fence and spacers
The secret to cutting precise dovetails on the band saw is to use an angled sled and spacers, as shown in the bottom photo. This sled slides back and forth along your rip fence to make the cuts to define the pins. Identical spacers are used to position the workpiece for each cut. An angled stop is glued to the back of the sled to position the workpiece at the desired angle (in our case, 14 degrees). Some experimentation will be needed to identify the size of the spacers required to fit the width of your workpiece.

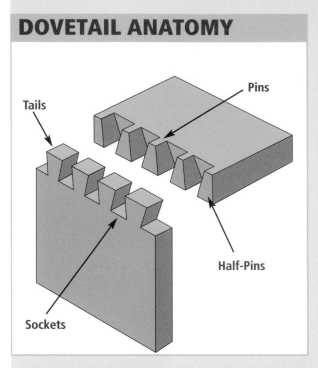

DOVETAIL ANATOMY

Tails

Pins

Half-Pins

Sockets

Make first tail cuts

Once you've made your angled sled and have cut your spacers to width, adjust the rip fence to define the first angled pin cut and lock it in place. Then with all the spacers in place, slide the sled forward until the blade reaches the line that you scribed earlier on the workpiece, as shown in the top photo.

Remove spacers and continue

Back the sled up until the blade is free from the workpiece. Remove the first spacer and slide the workpiece over. Then push the sled forward to make the next angled tail cut, as shown in the middle photo. Continue for the remaining angled cuts.

Make final cuts

Then back up the sled, flip the workpiece from side to side, and replace the spacers. Repeat the cutting procedure to define the other side of each tail. When you've cut both sides of the tails on one piece, switch to the next part and cut both sides of the tails; repeat for any remaining parts.

Remove half-pin waste

Once you've defined the sides of all of the tails, you can start to remove the waste between them. To prevent mistakes, it's a good idea to mark each waste section with an "X." This way you won't inadvertently remove a tail. Start by cutting away the half-pin waste on the end of each workpiece, as shown in the top photo. Stay to the waste side of the scribed line.

Remove waste between tails

Next, move on to removing the waste between the tails. Your best bet here is to install the narrowest blade that your band saw can handle. This will allow you to cut closer into the inside corners of each angled tail. If you use a wider blade, you can work your way toward the scribed line by making a series of angled cuts as shown in the middle photo. Here again, stay to the waste side of the scribed lines. Repeat this for all of the tail parts.

Set up for cutting pins

The pins can be cut using the same spacers that you used to cut the tails. The difference here is that you don't need the sled. All you have to do is angle your saw table to 14 degrees, as shown in the bottom photo, and set up your rip fence to locate the pins in the correct position. This will also take a bit of experimentation. That's why it's a good idea to fully cut one tail piece and check the fit in the tails before cutting all your pieces.

Define first half of pins

Just as you did with the dovetail sled, butt your spacers up against the rip fence and make your first angled cut to define one side of a pin. Then back out the workpiece, remove a spacer, and cut the next pin side. Repeat this for each of the pin pieces before proceeding to the next step.

Define second half of pins

If you're lucky enough to have a band saw where the table tilts both ways (like the Jet saw shown here; it tilts 15 degrees in one direction and 45 degrees in the other), cutting the second angled side of the pins is just a matter of tilting the table in the opposite direction 14 degrees and repeating the spacer block/cutting sequence. If your saw doesn't tilt the opposite way, you'll have to make an angled sled as described on page 56. Once you're set up, cut the second angled side on all the pin pieces as shown in the middle photo.

Remove the pin waste

As you did for the tail waste, mark each waste section between each pin with an "X" to prevent accidental removal. Unfortunately, the band saw can't easily handle the task of removing the waste between the pins, so you'll have to use a coping saw as shown in the bottom photo. Keep to the waste side of the scribed line, and remove the majority of the waste between the pins on all the pin pieces. Then break out your sharpest chisel and trim the spaces between the pins and the tails to the scribed line. Test the fit of each dovetail and trim as needed until the parts slide together smoothly.

5 Band Saw Jigs and Fixtures

Rarely does a day go by in the average shop when a woodworker doesn't reach for a jig or fixture to make a cut on a power tool. And the band saw is no exception to this. There are numerous jigs and fixtures that you can build for your band saw that can expand its usefulness in the workshop.

This chapter features a dozen jigs, including horizontal and vertical featherboards to increase the accuracy of your cuts, push sticks and push blocks to make cuts safer, and a band saw table and fence with attachments that dramatically increase the working area of your saw and provide an accurate way to rip and resaw stock, as well as improve your saw's joint-making capabilities. Finally, there is a circle-cutting jig, two types of resaw fences, and a unique sliding fence that lets you make your own lumber.

Cut your own lumber. Make perfect circles. And expand your band saw's ability to cut joints. These are just a few of the dozen jigs and fixtures featured in this chapter.

Featherboard

A featherboard is one of the best ways to both protect your fingers and also add precision to almost any cut made on the band saw. A featherboard has a set of flexible fingers at its end that when clamped against a workpiece will press the workpiece into the rip fence to ensure an accurate cut.

You can purchase featherboards or make your own. The shop-made version shown in the top left photo and illustrated in the drawing below right slides back and forth in the miter gauge slot and locks in place with a simple homemade clamp system. It's adjustable to handle a variety of stock widths and is both easy to make and easy to use.

Rout slot in blank

In order to position the featherboard over a wide range, a slot is cut in it to allow for adjustment. The slot is 1/4" wide and 3" long. The simplest way to cut this is to start by laying out the ends of the slot, then drill a 1/4" start and stop hole at each end of the slot. This way you can place one of the holes over a 1/4" straight bit fitted in a router or router table and slide the router table fence or edge guide on a portable router up against the featherboard. Then just turn on the router while keeping a firm grip on the featherboard and rout away the waste in between the limit holes to form

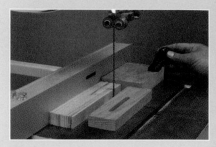

the slot, as shown in the top right photo (we used a clamp to safely hold the blank while routing). Alternatively, remove the waste by laying out the sides of the slot and cutting along these lines with a saber saw or coping saw.

Set up band saw fence and stop

You could cut the fingers for the featherboard on the band saw freehand, but odds are they won't end up uniform in width and so won't exert even pressure. To create uniform-width fingers, we set up the rip fence and a stop to limit the length (2") of the fingers as shown in the lower photo above. Then we used 1/8" spacers to position the blank for cutting the fingers as described on the opposite page.

FEATHERBOARD ANATOMY

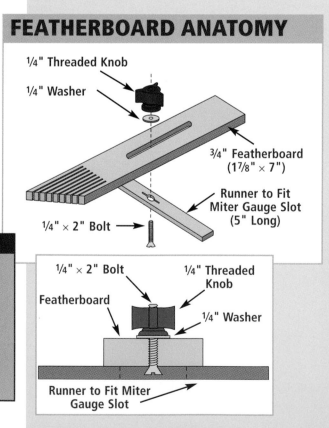

1/4" Threaded Knob

1/4" Washer

3/4" Featherboard (1 7/8" × 7")

Runner to Fit Miter Gauge Slot (5" Long)

1/4" × 2" Bolt

1/4" × 2" Bolt

1/4" Threaded Knob

Featherboard

1/4" Washer

Runner to Fit Miter Gauge Slot

MATERIALS LIST

Part	Quantity	Dimensions
Runner	1	3/4" × 5" – 1/2"
Featherboard	1	1 7/8" × 7" – 3/4"
Machine bolt	1	1/4" × 2"
Washer	1	1/4"
Threaded knob	1	1/4" threads

Cut kerfs using spacers

Cut a set of $1/8$"-thick spacers approximately $3/4$" wide and 7" long—you'll need 12 of them if you make your blank $1^7/8$" wide. Place all 12 spacers up against the rip fence and butt your blank against the spacers. Turn on the band saw and slide the blank forward into the blade until it hits the stop. Back out the blank, remove a spacer, and cut the second kerf as shown in the top photo. Repeat this procedure until you've cut all the kerfs. When done, cut the end of the fingers at a 15-degree angle.

Make the runner

The runner is cut to match the width and depth of your miter gauge slot. For most saws, this will be $1/2$" thick and $3/4$" wide; the runner is 5" long. The homemade clamp consists of a $1/4$" × 2" machine bolt, a $1/4$" washer, and a $1/4$" threaded knob. Here's how it works. The bolt fits in a countersunk hole centered on a short lengthwise slot that's cut in the runner. The bolt passes through the featherboard and a threaded knob is installed on the end. As the threaded knob is tightened, it pulls the bolt up, which forces the runner to expand in the miter gauge slot and lock it in place. Drill a $1/4$" hole centered on the width and length of the runner, as shown in the middle photo. Then countersink this so that the bolt head is flush with the face of the runner. Next cut a 2"-long kerf lengthwise in the runner centered on the hole. This can be done easily with a coping saw.

Assemble the featherboard

With all the parts complete, you can assemble the featherboard. Start by inserting the machine bolt through the hole in the runner. Then position the featherboard over the machine bolt. Slip on the $1/4$" washer and thread on the $1/4$" threaded knob to complete assembly as shown in the bottom photo.

To use the featherboard, first adjust your rip fence for the desired cut. Then butt the workpiece you'll be cutting up against the rip fence. Next, place the featherboard in the appropriate miter gauge slot. Loosen the threaded knob and slide the angled end of the featherboard over until it butts up against the workpiece. Now tighten the knob just so it's friction-tight. Remove the workpiece and slide the featherboard over about another $1/8$" and fully tighten

Vertical Featherboard

The standard featherboard described on pages 92–93 does a great job of pressing stock that's 1" or less in thickness against the rip fence. But many times you'll find that you'll be cutting thicker stock where it will only exert pressure near the bottom of your workpiece. For situations like this, you need a tall or vertical featherboard that will press the stock into the rip fence along its full thickness, or width if you're resawing. That's exactly what this featherboard, shown in the top photo and illustrated in the drawing below right, does, and it's simple to build and use.

Glue flexible finger to vertical support

The vertical featherboard consists of a base that holds a vertical support. A flexible finger is glued onto the vertical support to exert pressure on the workpiece. To make the vertical featherboard, start by cutting the pieces to size per the materials list below (one end of the base is mitered at 25 degrees). Then glue the flexible finger to the vertical support as shown in the middle photo.

VERTICAL FEATHERBOARD

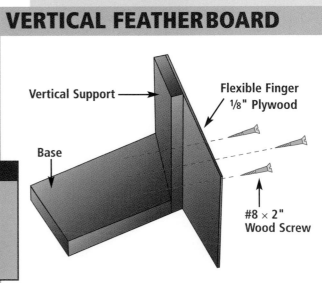

MATERIALS LIST

Part	Quantity	Dimensions
Base	1	$3\frac{3}{4}" \times 8" - \frac{3}{4}"$
Vertical support	1	$4" \times 5\frac{1}{4}" - \frac{3}{4}"$
Flexible finger	1	$5\frac{1}{4}" \times 8" - \frac{1}{8}"$

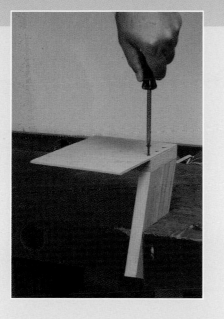

Attach support to base

All that's left is to attach the vertical support and flexible finger to the base as shown in the top photo. We used three #8 × 2"-long screws for this, spaced about 3/4" apart. Note that you'll need to install the first screw near the inside edge where the base meets the support, as shown in the top photo. This will prevent the third screw from protruding out of the base. When it's screwed together, gently sand a slight roundover on the vertical edges of the flexible finger.

USING THE VERTICAL FEATHERBOARD

As with any featherboard, you'll want to position the featherboard so the pressure from the finger (or fingers) is exerted on the workpiece slightly in front of the blade. If you were to position it at or behind the blade, all you'd accomplish is pinching the cut portion against the blade, which will create either a ragged cut or burned cut, or both.

Roughly position featherboard. To use the vertical featherboard, start by setting up the cut. Position the rip fence for the desired cut, and butt your workpiece up against the rip fence. Then roughly position the featherboard on your saw top and clamp it to the saw top so it's friction-tight as shown in the bottom left photo.

Adjust for flex. Now pivot the featherboard into the workpiece so that the flexible finger bows a bit, as shown in the bottom right photo. Keep the pressure on the flexible finger while fully tightening the clamps with your other hand. Now you're ready to make the cut. Back the workpiece out by temporarily bending the flexible finger away from the workpiece. Then turn on the saw and make the cut.

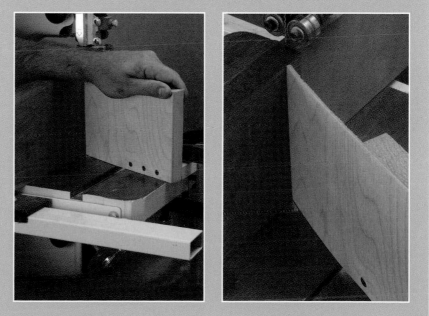

Push Block

The number one safety device you can use with a band saw is a push stick (see page 98) or a push block. Although there are numerous commercially made push blocks, the shop-made version shown here works just as well. The advantage of making your own from wood is if there's a slip and the push block comes in contact with the blade, there's no blade damage. The push block illustrated in the drawing below consists of a handle attached to a base that is kerfed at one end to hold a strip of 1/4" hardboard. In use, the base presses the workpiece firmly into the saw top or rip fence (as shown here) and the strip of hardboard hooks over the end of the workpiece so that you can safely push it forward.

Make the handle

To make the push block, start by cutting the pieces to size per the materials list below. Then lay out the handle pattern illustrated below on the handle blank. Next, cut this to shape on the band saw as shown in the middle photo. After cutting the handle to shape, soften the top edges for a comfortable fit by routing or sanding a 1/4" roundover.

PUSH BLOCK ANATOMY

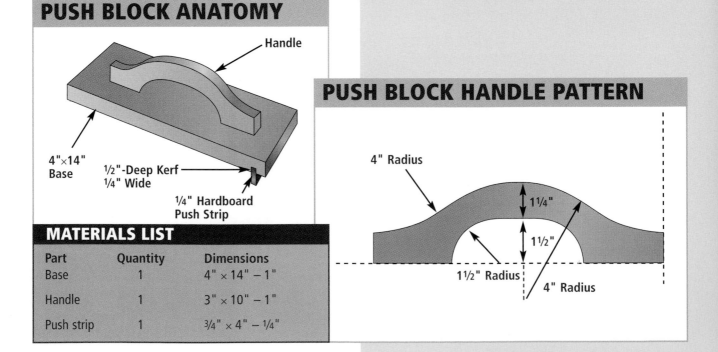

Handle

4"×14" Base

1/2"-Deep Kerf 1/4" Wide

1/4" Hardboard Push Strip

MATERIALS LIST

Part	Quantity	Dimensions
Base	1	4" × 14" – 1"
Handle	1	3" × 10" – 1"
Push strip	1	3/4" × 4" – 1/4"

PUSH BLOCK HANDLE PATTERN

4" Radius

1 1/4"

1 1/2"

1 1/2" Radius

4" Radius

Kerf the base

The kerf in the bottom of the base accepts the 1/4"-thick push strip. Since we wanted to be able to replace these strips in the future, they're not glued in place. Instead they're a friction-fit. With this in mind, you'll want to cut the kerf in the base so it's just a hair narrower than the thickness of the push strip material. Cut the kerf in the base roughly 1/2" deep, as shown in the top photo. The kerf is roughly 3/4" in from the end of the base.

Attach the handle

With the base kerfed, you can attach the handle with screws. You can screw it to the base either from above, as shown in the middle photo, or from underneath. In either case, make sure to choose a screw length that will not protrude out of the base or handle.

Add the push strip

All that's left is to press a push strip into the kerf in the base, as shown in the bottom photo. If in time the fit becomes loose, you can add paper shims or masking tape to create a snug fit. It's also a good idea to cut a few extra push strips and keep them on hand in case the old strip gets dinged up or damaged.

Push Stick

It's simple. If you don't want to cut your fingers when using a band saw—use a push stick to push the workpiece past the blade. Push sticks come in a wide variety of shapes and sizes. You can purchase them or make your own. The push stick shown in the top photo is easy to make and can be readily replaced if

by chance it hits the blade. It can be made from 1/2"- or 3/4"-thick scrap stock. Solid wood is fine, but plywood, with its cross-banded layers, will prove to be stronger over time. A half-sized pattern for the push stick is illustrated below. Note that there's a notch up high on the handle of the stick. This notch helps prevent your hand from sliding down if the workpiece catches on something.

Consider making a template for this useful accessory. Enlarge the half-sized pattern and transfer this to template stock with carbon paper, or make a 200% copy and attach it with spray-on adhesive or rubber cement. Cut out the template and use this to lay out the push stick on your plywood scrap. You can get two push blocks out of a single 3"-wide by 13"-long scrap.

Cut out the shape

Now you can cut out the push stick(s) as shown in the middle photo. Take your time and keep to the waste side of the layout lines. Err on the side of making the stick thicker and not thinner, to keep it stout enough to push heavy stock. Consider making a set in three thicknesses: 1/4", 1/2", and 3/4" so you can fit the push stick between the rip fence and the saw blade when ripping a variety of stock widths.

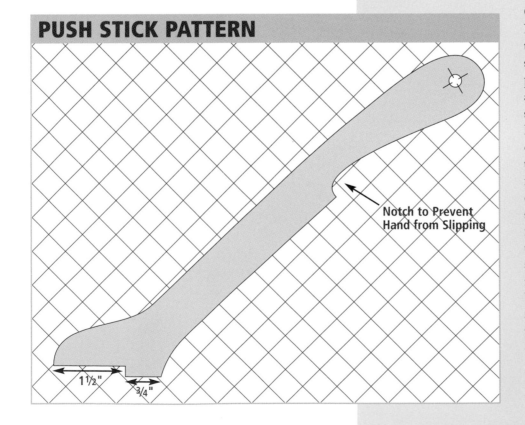

PUSH STICK PATTERN

Notch to Prevent Hand from Slipping

1 1/2"

3/4"

Band Saw Table

Just like a drill press, the table on a typical band saw is way too small. Manufacturers tend to make them small to keep costs down. Unfortunately, this means you have to struggle often to support a workpiece properly when making a cut. The band saw table shown here is designed for the Delta ShopMaster saw and effectively doubles the size of the table (but it can be modified to fit most any saw). What's more, it also creates perfectly flat and parallel front and back edges, which can be used with the shop-made fence and attachments described on pages 103–111. Additionally, since the table extends out past the original cast table and is uniform thickness, it's much easier to clamp accessories onto its edges—which is a real hassle on cast-iron or aluminum tops, as the ribs of the casting frequently interfere with clamp heads or pads.

The band saw table shown here is made up of a top, a side guide, and a front stop, as illustrated in the drawing at right. In use, the saw table slides onto your saw top and is guided by the side guide under its left edge. Just push the table forward until the front stop contacts the front edge of your saw table and lock the table in place with the built-in cams. The cams press up against the right edge of the saw table to capture the top between the side guide and the cams.

To build the band saw table, start by determining the size of the table you want. In most cases if you double the surface area of the existing table, you'll end up with plenty of support for most cutting jobs. You'll also need to determine the width and length of the side guide and front stop. These should be sized to roughly center the table on the saw blade.

BAND SAW TABLE ANATOMY

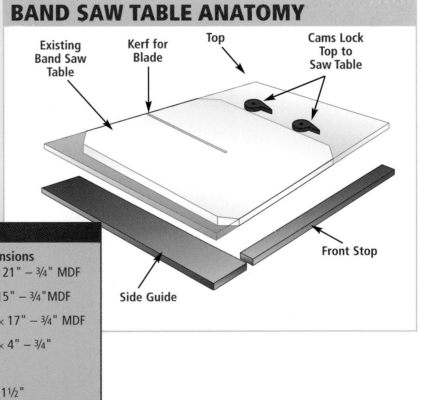

Existing Band Saw Table

Kerf for Blade

Top

Cams Lock Top to Saw Table

Front Stop

Side Guide

MATERIALS LIST

Part	Quantity	Dimensions
Top	1	15" × 21" – 3/4" MDF
Side guide	1	4" × 15" – 3/4" MDF
Front stop	1	1 1/2" × 17" – 3/4" MDF
Cams	2	1 1/2" × 4" – 3/4"
Inserts	2	1/4"
Bolts	2	1/4" × 1 1/2"
Washers	2	1/4"

Attach side guide and front stop

Once you've determined the dimensions for your top, side guide, and front stop, cut them to size. Then glue them to the underside of the top as shown in the top photo. Fasteners are not really required here, as there's plenty of surface area for a good glue bond. However, if you don't have tons of clamps, you can use screws to hold the parts in place until the glue dries.

Kerf the top

When the glue has set, the next step is to cut a kerf in the top so you can slide it on and off the saw table. To do this, simply turn on the saw and butt the side guide up against the left edge of your saw table. Push the top forward, maintaining constant contact between the side guide and the saw table until the front stop makes contact with the front edge of the saw table, as shown in the middle photo. Turn off the saw and back out the top. Repeat this procedure a couple of times to create a slightly wider kerf that will make it easy to slide the top on and off without catching on the saw blade.

Locate the cams

At this point, you could use the top as is by clamping it to the saw table. But clamps are cumbersome and frequently get in the way of your workpiece during a cut. We chose to lock the top to the saw table with cams. To locate the cams on the underside of the top, position the top on the tabel so the front stop contacts the saw table. Then trace a line on the bottom of the top to define the location of the saw table as shown in the bottom photo.

Drill holes for inserts

The cams that lock the top in place are attached to the underside of the saw table via a pair of $1/4$" bolts that thread into $1/4$" threaded inserts driven or screwed into the underside of the saw top, as illustrated in the bottom drawing. In our case, we located the holes for the inserts 4" and 10" in from the front edge of the saw top and 1" to the right of the line marked previously. Lay out and centerpunch these holes. Then drill the recommended-sized holes for your inserts as shown in the top photo, taking care not to break through the top.

Install the inserts

Now you can install the inserts. We used the type that are pounded in place with a hammer as shown in the middle photo. Alternatively, you can use the type that thread in. Whichever type you use, make sure that each insert is installed slightly below the surface so that the cam can be pulled down tightly against the top with the cam bolts.

CAM/TABLETOP CROSS SECTION

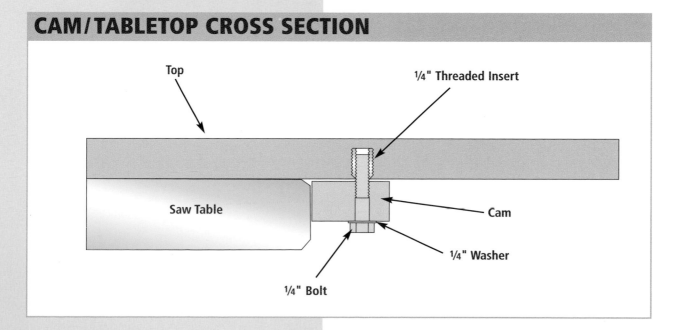

Top

$1/4$" Threaded Insert

Saw Table

Cam

$1/4$" Washer

$1/4$" Bolt

Cut out the cams

All that's left is to cut out and install the cams. Copy the full-sized pattern illustrated in the drawing below onto a blank large enough for two cams. Then cut them to shape on the band saw as shown in the top photo. Hardwood works well for these, but a premium plywood (as shown here) does a good job, too, as the many cross-banded layers of veneer create a strong handle as well as a stout cam. Sand the edges of the cams smooth and drill holes as shown for the cam bolts.

Install the cams

Finally, you can install the cams underneath the table by threading bolts with washers through the holes in the cams and into the inserts, as shown in the middle photo. A couple of things here. First, you'll likely need to sand a slight flat on the edge of the cam where it contacts the fence to help it snap or "toggle" into place. If you omit this step, the cams can apply pressure but will likely loosen due to saw vibration. Second, you may want to add a drop or two of Loctite adhesive into the inserts to prevent the cam bolts from vibrating loose during a cut.

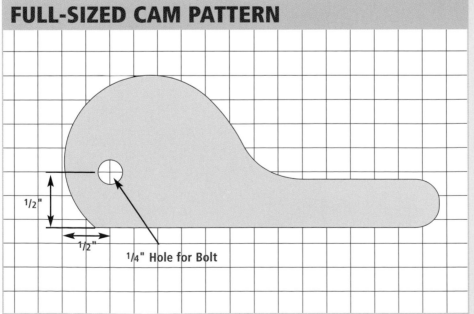

FULL-SIZED CAM PATTERN

1/2"

1/2"

1/4" Hole for Bolt

Band Saw Fence

A rip fence is an essential accessory for the band saw. It allows you to do so much more with the tool. Operations like ripping, resawing, and joint making all need a rip fence. Although you can purchase a ready-made rip fence—and there are

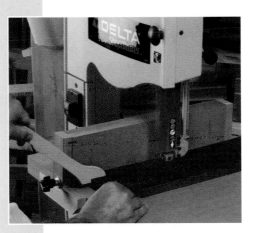

some very nice ones out there—they're not inexpensive. The rip fence shown here can handle many of the same tasks as a commercial rip fence for a fraction of the cost—a few scraps of wood and a couple dollars of hardware, and you've got a fence that's easy to use and reliable. We liked this fence so much that we designed a couple of nifty attachments to use with it: a narrow stock fence that doubles as a stop (see pages 108–109) and a single-point resaw attachment for resawing (see pages 110–111).

The rip fence shown here and illustrated in the drawing above fits the table shown on pages 99–102, but it can be modified to fit almost any saw top with smooth and parallel front and back edges. Our rip fence consists of a fence made up of a double layer of 3/4" MDF. A threaded rod runs through the body of the fence and passes through a fixed back cleat and an adjustable front cleat and bracket. Tightening a knob on the end of the threaded rod pulls the back cleat toward the front cleat and bracket to lock the fence in place on the saw top.

BAND SAW FENCE ANATOMY

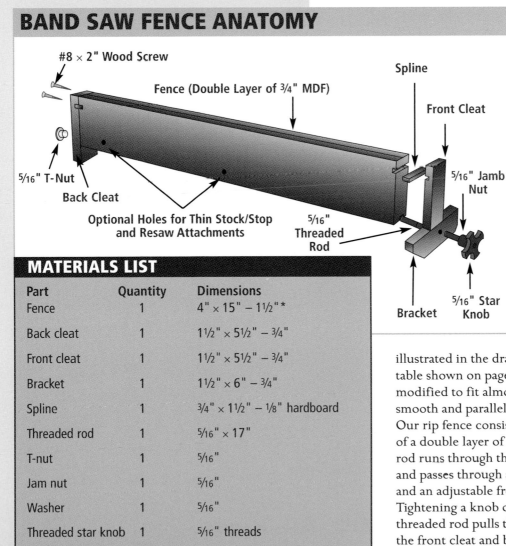

MATERIALS LIST

Part	Quantity	Dimensions
Fence	1	4" × 15" – 1½"*
Back cleat	1	1½" × 5½" – 3/4"
Front cleat	1	1½" × 5½" – 3/4"
Bracket	1	1½" × 6" – 3/4"
Spline	1	3/4" × 1½" – 1/8" hardboard
Threaded rod	1	5/16" × 17"
T-nut	1	5/16"
Jam nut	1	5/16"
Washer	1	5/16"
Threaded star knob	1	5/16" threads

*double layer of 3/4"-thick MDF

Make the fence body

To make the rip fence, first determine the length of the fence by measuring from front to back on your saw table. Cut two pieces of MDF (medium-density fiberboard) to this length and a width to match the maximum cutting capacity of your saw. Then glue these two pieces together as shown in the top photo, taking care to keep the edges flush.

Groove body for threaded rod

Allow the glue to set, and then scrape off any residue. Check to make sure the sides of the fence are perfectly perpendicular to the top and bottom. If they're not, or the edges of the two pieces aren't flush, then joint, plane, or sand them as needed. Then cut a $3/8" \times 3/8"$-wide groove the length of the fence centered on its width, as shown in the middle photo. This groove is for the threaded rod that will be added later.

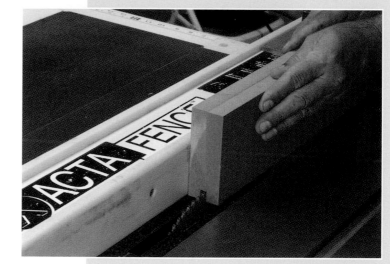

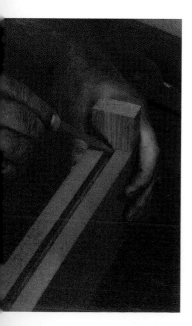

Locate the hole in the back cleat

Cut a front and a back cleat to a width of $1^1/2"$ and the height of your fence plus $1^1/2"$. Set one cleat aside for the front bracket and butt the other cleat up against the end of the fence as shown in the bottom photo, with the groove in the fence facing up. Then use a pencil to mark the groove location on the back of the cleat, as shown, to locate the hole that the threaded rod will pass through.

Drill holes and install T-nut

Once you've located the hole in the back cleat, drill a 3/8" hole and then install a T-nut on the back side of the cleat as shown in the top photo. Depending on your T-nut, you may need to enlarge the hole slightly to provide clearance for the barrel of the T-nut.

Attach the back cleat

Now you can drill a pair of countersunk pilot holes 1" down from the top edge and 3/8" in from each side edge for the screws that will hold the back cleat to the fence body. Position the back cleat on the fence body so the hole in the cleat aligns with the groove in the fence, and drill pilot holes through the cleat and into the MDF. It's essential that you drill full-length pilot holes in the edges of MDF or it'll split along its thickness when you drive in the screws. With the pilot holes drilled, attach the cleat to the fence with screws as shown in the middle photo.

BAND SAW FENCE DETAILS

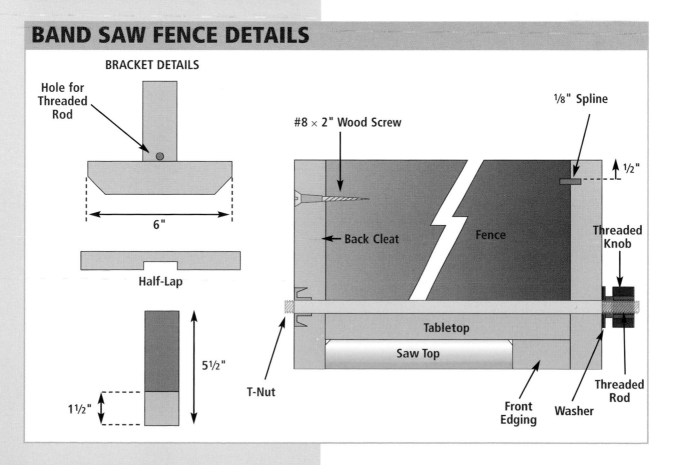

BRACKET DETAILS

Hole for Threaded Rod

6"

Half-Lap

5½"

1½"

1/8" Spline

#8 × 2" Wood Screw

½"

Back Cleat

Fence

Threaded Knob

Threaded Rod

T-Nut

Tabletop

Saw Top

Front Edging

Washer

Cut half-laps for fence bracket

The two parts of the fence bracket, the front cleat and bracket, are joined together with half-laps. One half of the joint is cut on the end of the front cleat and the other half of the joint is cut in the middle of the bracket, as shown in the top photo. Although we cut these on the table saw, you can also cut them on the band saw as described on page 81; note that the centered half-lap can be cut like one half of the faux mortise as described on pages 84–85.

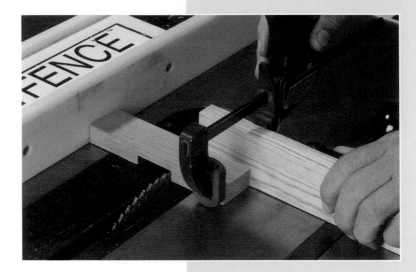

Assemble the bracket

With both halves of the half-lap cut, join the two parts together with glue and clamps as shown in the middle photo.

Kerf parts for spline

The fence bracket connects to the fence by way of a spline that fits in kerfs cut in the fence body and the front cleat. Set up your table saw to create a $1/8$"-wide kerf $1/2$" from the rip fence. The depth of the kerf should be $3/8$". Now you can cut a kerf on each part. Cut one kerf near the top of the fence on the end as shown in the bottom photo. Cut the other kerf on the inside face of the front cleat near its top, as shown in the bottom inset photo.

Locate hole in front bracket

Just as you did with the back cleat, you'll need to locate a hole in the fence bracket for the threaded rod to pass through. To do this, first cut a spline to size and insert it in the kerfs you just cut in the front cleat and fence body. Then hold the fence bracket in place and use a pencil to mark the hole location as shown in the top photo. Now you can centerpunch and drill a $3/8$" hole.

Attach knob onto threaded rod

Measure from the front to the back cleat, add 1" to this, and cut a piece of $5/16$" threaded rod to this length. Then thread a $5/16$" nut onto one end of the rod and thread on the threaded knob. Use a wrench to lock the jam nut against the inside face of the knob as shown in the middle photo.

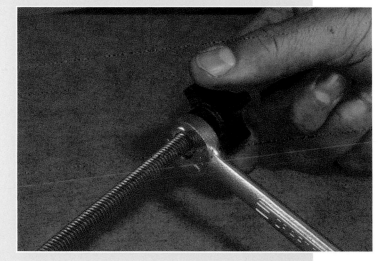

Assemble the fence

All that's left to assemble the fence is to thread the threaded rod through the fence bracket and groove in the fence body. Then thread the rod through the back cleat and into the T-nut as shown in the bottom photo. Place the fence on the table or saw top and test the clamping action. You may need to trim the fence body or widen the spline to get the proper grip. When tightened, there should be no side-to-side play of the fence body at all.

Narrow Stock/Stop Attachment

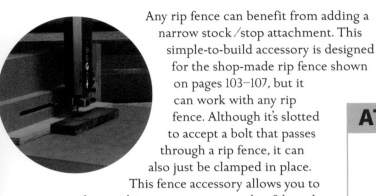

Any rip fence can benefit from adding a narrow stock/stop attachment. This simple-to-build accessory is designed for the shop-made rip fence shown on pages 103–107, but it can work with any rip fence. Although it's slotted to accept a bolt that passes through a rip fence, it can also just be clamped in place. This fence accessory allows you to do two things: cut narrow stock safely and also limit cuts by serving as a stop.

Whenever you go to cut a narrow work-piece, you'll find that a standard rip fence will not allow you to lower the upper guide assembly down far enough to cover the blade. That's because it'll hit the rip fence. The narrow stock fence extends its base away from the rip fence so you can lower the guide assembly as shown in the top left photo. In the stop mode, the attachment fits onto the rip fence behind the blade and is adjustable over a wide range, as shown in the top right photo.

The narrow stock/stop attachment is made up of two parts that are glued together: a slotted cleat and a base. It attaches to your rip fence via a carriage bolt that slides in the slotted cleat and passes through a hole or holes drilled in the rip fence. A knob threads onto the carriage bolt to lock the attachment in the desired position.

ATTACHMENT EXPLODED VIEW

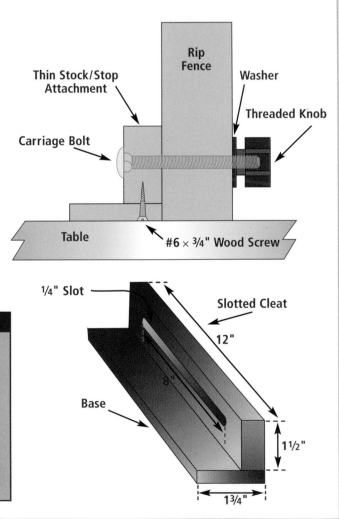

Thin Stock/Stop Attachment

Rip Fence

Washer

Threaded Knob

Carriage Bolt

Table

#6 × ³⁄₄" Wood Screw

¹⁄₄" Slot

Slotted Cleat

12"

8"

Base

1¹⁄₂"

1³⁄₄"

MATERIALS LIST

Part	Quantity	Dimensions
Slotted cleat	1	1¹⁄₂" × 12" – ³⁄₄"
Base	1	1³⁄₄" × 12" – ¹⁄₄"
Carriage bolt	1	¹⁄₄" × 2¹⁄₂"*
Washer	1	¹⁄₄"
Threaded knob	1	¹⁄₄" threads

*size to fit your rip fence

Slot the cleat

To make the narrow stock/stop attachment, begin by cutting the parts to size per the materials list. Unless your rip fence and saw top are much larger than the shop-built table shown on pages 99-102, the dimensions given here will work fine. If desired, though, you can lengthen these pieces as needed. If you're going to just clamp the attachment to your fence, proceed to the next step. If you want to attach it with a carriage bolt as described here, you'll need to slot the cleat. To do this, drill start and stop holes in the cleat and set one hole over a 1/4" straight bit mounted in a router or table-mounted router. Cut the slot in a series of light passes. It's a good idea to hold the narrow strip with a clamp as shown in the top photo.

Attach cleat to base

Now you can attach the cleat to the base with glue and clamps as shown in the middle photo. Allow the glue to completely dry before using the attachment.

Drill holes in fence and attach

All that's left is to drill holes in your rip fence for the carriage bolt to pass through. We drilled two holes: one located at the front edge of the teeth of the blade (as shown in the bottom photo), and one near the back of the fence. The front hole is used in the narrow stock mode and is also used for the single-point resaw attachment shown on pages 110–111. Place your attachment against the rip fence to locate how far up the holes should be from the bottom edge of your rip fence. The rear hole is used in the stop mode and should be located so that the end of the stop can be adjusted forward to touch the back of the blade. With the holes drilled, you can attach the fence/stop to your rip fence by threading the carriage bolt through the attachment and rip fence and threading on the knob, as shown in the bottom inset photo.

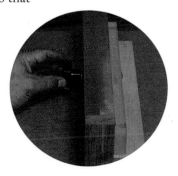

Single-Point Resaw Attachment

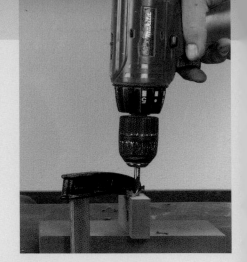

One of the challenges of resawing—dealing with blade lead or "drift"—can be easily overcome by using a single-point resaw fence as described on page 74. You can make a stand-alone version of one of these as described on pages 118–119, or you can make an attachment to fit your existing rip fence like the one shown in the top left photo. Although this attachment is designed to fit the shop-made fence shown on pages 103–107, it can be modified to fit almost any rip fence, as long as you're willing to drill a hole in your rip fence for the connector bolt that secures the attachment to the rip fence.

The single-point resaw attachment is just a single piece of wood with its edges rounded over to create a stable yet easy-to-use pivot point for resawing. The attachment is secured to your rip fence by way of a connector bolt that passes through the rip fence and into the attachment, and threads into a barrel nut, as illustrated in bottom drawing. The attachment itself is a piece of 1 1/2"-wide wood (MDF in our case) that's cut to match your fence height.

Drill connector screw hole

Once you've cut the attachment to size, the next step is to drill the hole for the 1/4" connector bolt. If you've already drilled a hole in your fence, you'll want to locate the hole in the attachment to match this. After you've located how far up from the bottom the hole needs to be, scribe a line centered on the thickness of the attachment and drill a stopped hole as shown in the top right photo. Since we located the barrel nut 1" in from the edge, we drilled our hole 1 1/4" deep to provide clearance for the end of the connector bolt.

MATERIALS LIST

Part	Quantity	Dimensions
Attachment	1	1 1/2" × 4" – 3/4"
Connector bolt	1	1/4" × 2 1/2"*
Connector nut	1	1/4" barrel bolt

*size to fit your rip fence

ATTACHMENT EXPLODED VIEW

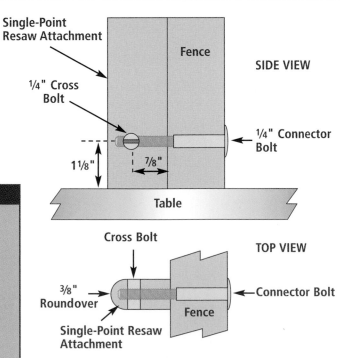

Single-Point Resaw Attachment

Fence

SIDE VIEW

1/4" Cross Bolt

1/4" Connector Bolt

1 1/8"   7/8"

Table

Cross Bolt

TOP VIEW

3/8" Roundover

Connector Bolt

Single-Point Resaw Attachment

Fence

Drill hole for barrel nut

Next, you can lay out and drill the intersecting hole for the barrel nut. We located this hole 1" in from the edge and located it to intersect the hole drilled for the connector bolt previously. For the barrel nut we used, we drilled a

³/₈"-diameter hole, as shown in the top photo. Check the packaging of the barrel nut you're using for the recommended-size hole.

Round over edges

To complete the attachment, round over the vertical edges to provide a smooth pivot point. You can sand, file, or rout these. If you do plan on routing this roundover, it's best to hold the small attachment with a clamp that can serve as a handle to safely rout the edges, as shown in the middle photo.

Attach to fence

The attachment connects to your rip fence with the connector bolt that passes through the rip fence and attachment and threads into the barrel nut. The length of the bolt should equal the thickness of your rip fence plus 1". Depending on the thickness of your rip fence, you may need to cut a longer connector bolt down to achieve this length. The advantage of using a connector bolt (commonly used in ready-to-assemble furniture) is that its large head provides a large surface area, which results in a firm grip. Most connector bolts use an Allen wrench to tighten or loosen them, as shown in the bottom photo.

Circle-Cutting Jig

With the aid of a circle-cutting jig like the one shown in the top photo, you can cut perfect circles on the band saw. Custom-cut any size wheels for toys or mobile furniture or make a round table top—even a round picture frame. For a circle-cutting jig to be useful, it must be easy to use and adjustable over a wide range.

To make our jig easy to use, the table of the jig is grooved to accept a runner that fits into the miter gauge slot on your saw top, as illustrated in the drawing at right. A dovetail-shaped slide fits into a dovetailed groove in the top. The slide holds a pivot pin on one end and is slotted along its length to make it adjustable. The slide is locked in place via a machine screw that passes through the slide and into a T-nut attached to the underside of the tabletop.

In use, you drill a hole in the bottom of a blank to fit over the pivot pin. A stop is attached to the front of the table to stop the table at the exact point where the pivot pin is in line with the blade. Then all

you do is rotate the blank on the pivot pin to cut a perfect circle. The dimensions in the materials list is for a jig designed to fit a Hitachi band saw. Modify the dimensions as needed to fit your saw.

CIRCLE-CUTTING JIG ANATOMY

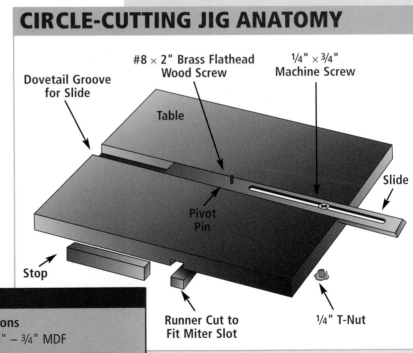

MATERIALS LIST

Part	Quantity	Dimensions
Table	1	13" × 16" − 3/4" MDF
Runner	1	3/4" × 13" − 1/2"
Stop	1	5/8" × 2 1/2" − 3/4"
Slide	1	1 1/8" × 12" − 1/4" hardboard
Pivot pin	1	#8 × 2" brass wood screw
Screw	1	1/4" × 3/4" flathead machine screw
T-nut	1	1/4"

Cut groove in top for runner

To make the circle-cutting jig, start by cutting the table to size. Then locate the groove for the runner on the underside of the table. Cut the groove on the table saw or with a router to match the width of your miter gauge slot, as shown in the top photo. In our case, the groove is 5/8" wide and 1/4" deep and it starts 6 1/2" in from the left edge of the table.

Rout dovetail slot for slide

The next step is to cut the dovetail groove in the top of the table to accept the slide. This is most easily done with a dovetail bit and a router, as shown in the middle photo. Our groove is 1 1/8" wide (from angled corner to angled corner) and is 1/4" deep. The reason we used a dovetail groove is that the angled sides of the groove trap the angled sides of the slide in place and keep it from lifting up—something that can't be achieved with a plain groove.

Glue in the runner

With all the grooves cut into the table, you can cut a runner to fit and glue it in place as shown in the bottom photo. You're looking for a runner that fits snug in the miter gauge slot with no side-to-side play, but will still slide smoothly.

Cut dovetail slide

Now you can turn your attention to the slide, as illustrated in the drawing on the opposite page. The first thing to do is to bevel-rip one edge of a piece of $1/4$" hardboard to match the angle of the dovetail bit you used to cut the groove. Then flip the hardboard or tilt the saw blade to cut an opposite angle to the first beveled edge. Set the rip fence on your table to create a $1^1/8$"-wide slide and bevel-rip the slide to width, as shown in the top photo.

Rout slot in slide

To make the slide adjustable, you'll need to cut an 8"-long slot centered along its length, 1" in from one end. The easiest way to do this is to lay out the start and stop points of the slot and drill $1/4$" holes at these points. Then set the fence on your router table fitted with a $1/4$" straight bit to cut a centered groove. Grip the narrow slide with a clamp as shown in the middle photo, and rout the slot. Alternatively, you can drill the start/stop holes and pencil in the slot between the holes and remove the waste with a coping saw.

Chamfer the slot

Since the head of the flathead machine screw you'll use to lock the slide in place has angled sides, you'll need to angle the slides of the slot to allow it to sit below the surface of the slide—something it has to do in order not to interfere with the blank that will sit on top of the slide and table. There are a number of ways to do this. You can simply sand or file the edges at an angle, or chamfer the slot in a single pass using a V-groove bit mounted in the router table as shown in the bottom photo. Note that if you do this, you'll want to use a grout float (as shown here) or other push block that can exert downward pressure on the slide as it is pushed forward over the spinning bit.

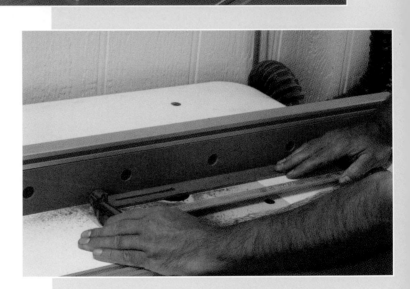

Drive in the T-nut

With the bottom of the table prepared for the T-nut, drive it in place with a hammer as shown in the photo at right.

Locate the hole for the T-nut

With the slide slotted and chamfered, you can use it to locate the hole in the table for the machine screw and T-nut that lock it in place. Push the slide into the groove and slide it over until its end is flush with the edge of the table, as shown in the top left photo. Then use a pencil to mark the end of the slot on the groove bottom as shown.

Drill the holes for the T-nut

Once you've located the hole, centerpunch its location and drill a ¼" hole through the table, as shown in the the inset photo below. Then flip the table over and drill a counterbore to fit the T-nut you're using, as shown in the photo at left. Note that you may have to enlarge the hole slightly to accept the barrel of the T-nut.

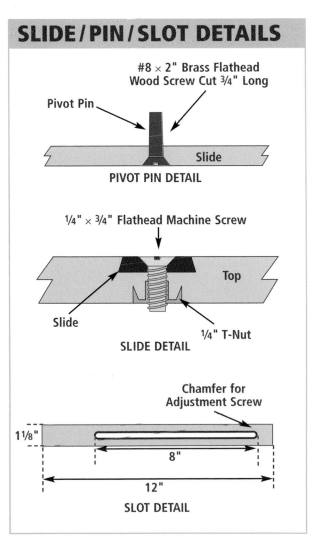

SLIDE/PIN/SLOT DETAILS

#8 × 2" Brass Flathead Wood Screw Cut ¾" Long

Pivot Pin

Slide

PIVOT PIN DETAIL

¼" × ¾" Flathead Machine Screw

Top

Slide

¼" T-Nut

SLIDE DETAIL

Chamfer for Adjustment Screw

1⅛"

8"

12"

SLOT DETAIL

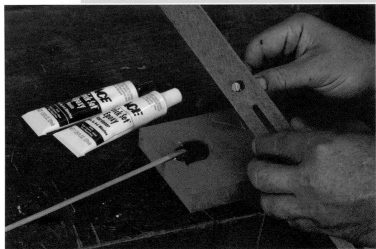

Drill hole for the pivot pin

To complete the slide, the final step is to install the pivot pin. This pin is nothing more than a #8 × 2" brass flathead wood screw with the threads cut off. We used brass because the softer metal tends less to enlarge the pivot pin hole drilled in the underside of the blank than do pins made of harder metals. Locate the pin about 1" from the blade with the table in place on the saw top. This will allow you to cut 2"-diameter wheels and larger. Once you've located the pin, drill a hole to accept the shank of the pin as shown in the top right photo. Then flip the slide over and drill a countersink for the head of the screw as shown in the top left photo.

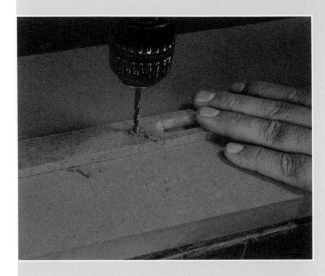

Epoxy the pin in place

To prevent the pivot pin from working loose in the slide, it's a good idea to epoxy it in place. First cut the pivot pin to length (we cut ours about 5/8" to 3/4" long). Mix up a small amount of epoxy and apply a dollop to the countersunk hole in the underside of the slide. Don't use a lot here; otherwise you'll end up with epoxy on the pivot pin and possibly on the top of the table. Insert the pin in the hole as shown in the middle photo, and push it in until the head bottoms out in the countersunk hole. Wipe off any excess epoxy immediately.

Insert the slide

When the epoxy has cured completely, insert the slide in the dovetailed groove in the table and thread the machine screw through the slide and into the T-nut as shown in the bottom photo. Check to make sure it slides smoothly and locks in place as it's tightened. The angled sides of the screw head should force the chamfered sides of the slot out to firmly lock the slide in the groove.

■ USING THE CIRCLE JIG

Before you can use the circle jig to cut circles, there's one more thing to do: locate and install the stop that limits the forward travel of the table. To do this, place the jig on the saw table with its runner engaged in the miter gauge slot. Then turn on your saw and slide the jig slowly forward until the pivot pin is in direct line with the teeth of the saw blade. Stop pushing the jig and turn off the saw. Mark the underside of the front top edge to define the location of the saw stop. Then install the stop so its front edge is flush with the line you just drew. This will stop the table at the exact place for circle cutting every time.

Set sliding arm for desired radius. When you're ready to cut a circle, start by positioning the slide for the desired radius as shown in the photo at right. We find that laying a metal rule on the table so its end touches the blade as shown is an easy way to do this.

Prepare the blank. Next, you'll need to prepare the blank. Start by locating the center of the blank by drawing opposing diagonals. Then center-punch this location and drill a hole to match the diameter of your pivot pin, as shown in the inset photo at left. Note the use of a simple depth gauge—the masking tape—to prevent from drilling through the blank. Now flip the blank over and insert it onto the pivot pin as shown in the photo at right.

Slide forward and rotate. With the blank prepared, you can cut the circle. Turn on your saw and push the jig forward until the stop contacts the front edge of your saw table as shown in the inset photo at left. Then just rotate the blank as shown in the photo at right 360 degrees to cut the circle.

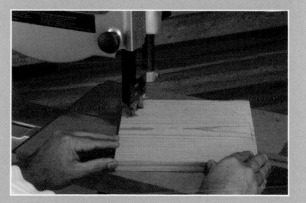

Single-Point Resaw Fence

Blade lead or "drift" is a problem you'll encounter on every band saw blade you use. Drift is caused by the uneven set of the teeth of the saw. If you've ever used a handsaw that was difficult to keep on track for a straight cut, you've experienced drift. Basically, the uneven set tends to pull or push the workpiece in one direction—sort of like a car in need of a front-end alignment.

Drift is a major concern whenever you use a rip fence to guide a workpiece—especially when resawing. If the drift causes the workpiece to angle away from the fence, you end up with a tapered workpiece. When it forces the workpiece into the fence, the cut may be accurate, but the edges are often rough and it's typically more difficult to push the workpiece forward, as the drift causes the workpiece to bind against the fence.

One way to get around this is to identify the drift and angle your rip fence accordingly, as described on page 51. Another method to compensate for drift is to replace the rip fence with a single-point contact fence. A single-point fence like the one shown in the top photo makes it easy for you to angle the piece as you cut to compensate for drift while still producing a cut that's uniform in thickness. That's because you position a single point away from the blade the desired

thickness of the finished workpiece. The single-point fence we designed is sturdy and easy to build and use. It consists of four pieces: a fence, two supports. and a clamping base, as illustrated in the drawing below. Our fence is designed for most 14" band saws with a 6" maximum cut capacity, but you can modify its height as needed to fit your saw.

Rout the roundovers

Start by cutting the single-point fence pieces to size as described in the materials list (modify the height if necessary). Then round over both vertical edges of the fence and one vertical edge of each support. We did this with a ⅜" roundover bit in a table-mounted router, as shown in the middle right photo. But you could just as easily do this with a file or sandpaper.

SINGLE-POINT RESAW FENCE ANATOMY

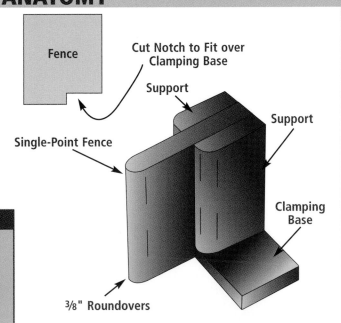

Fence

Cut Notch to Fit over Clamping Base

Support

Support

Single-Point Fence

Clamping Base

⅜" Roundovers

MATERIALS LIST

Part	Quantity	Dimensions
Fence	1	6" × 6" − ¾"
Supports	2	3" × 6" − ¾"
Clamping base	1	3" × 6" − ¾"

Cut a notch in the fence

Next, a notch needs to be cut in the inside bottom corner of the fence to allow it to fit over the clamping base. Hold one end of the base against the fence and scribe around it with a pencil to define the notch. Then cut the notch out on the band saw as shown in the top left photo.

Assemble the fence

Now you can start assembling the fence. Do this by first attaching the clamping base centered onto the fence with glue and screws as shown in the middle photo. If you're using MDF as shown here, it's important to drill full-length pilot holes in the fence before driving in screws, or you'll split the MDF along its thickness. With the base attached, you can glue the supports onto each side of the fence as shown in the inset photo above.

Setting up for a cut

To use the single-point fence, start by roughly positioning it in line with the saw blade as shown in the bottom right photo. Clamp the fence to your saw table friction-tight, and adjust the gap between the fence and the blade for the desired cut. You want the tip of the roundover to be in line with the teeth of the blade. Tighten the clamps fully and make your cut. Note: It's best to strike a cut line along the edge of the workpiece to serve as a reference as you cut; angle the workpiece as needed to keep the workpiece on track with the blade.

Slip-On Resaw Fence

Resawing a board requires that the board be held on edge for the cut. Keeping the bottom edge flat on the saw top and not tilting the workpiece one way or the other can be a real challenge, especially when resawing stock less than 1" in thickness. A tall fence attached to your rip fence will provide the much-needed support to make this less of a challenge. The only problem with a tall fence used for resawing is that you can't attach it to your fence with clamps because the clamps will get in the way. This means that you either need to build a separate tall fence (as described on page 73) or screw the tall fence to your existing rip fence—and if your rip fence doesn't have holes in it for this, you'll have to drill a set.

Our solution is a slip-on fence that fits over your fence and extends up to provide additional support,

as shown in the top left photo. Because it slips on and off, there's no hassle with dealing with screws. The slip-on fence shown here is designed to fit over the fence supplied with the Ryobi band saw, but you can modify the dimensions as needed to fit over any fence. The slip-on fence is made up of three parts: a tall fence, a top, and a side, as illustrated in the drawing below left. If necessary, optional braces can be added as well.

Determine the fence height

To make the slip-on fence, begin by determining the height of the fence. Adjust the upper guide assembly on your saw to its highest position. Then measure the distance between the bottom of the guide assembly and the saw table as shown in the top right photo. Cut the fence to this and to match the length of your fence.

Locate the groove for the top

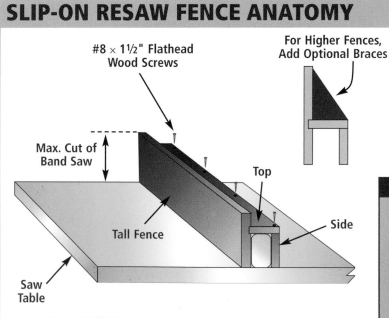

Next, butt the tall fence up against your rip fence (as shown in the photo at right) and trace along the top of the fence to locate the bottom of the groove you'll cut for the top. Then cut a 3/4"-wide, 1/4"-deep groove the length of the fence for the top.

SLIP-ON RESAW FENCE ANATOMY

#8 × 1½" Flathead Wood Screws

For Higher Fences, Add Optional Braces

Max. Cut of Band Saw

Top

Tall Fence

Side

Saw Table

MATERIALS LIST

Part	Quantity	Dimensions
Tall fence	1	4" × 16" – 3/4"
Top	1	2⅜" × 16" – 3/4"
Side	1	2½" × 16" – 3/4"
Braces	4	(optional; see text)

Glue the top to the fence

Once you've cut the groove for the top, you can cut the top to size and glue it in the groove. The top is the same width as your rip fence plus $1/4$". Apply glue in the groove and clamp the top in place as shown in the top photo. When the glue has dried, butt the tall fence up against your fence and measure from the underside of the top to the saw top, and cut a side to this dimension and to match the length of your rip fence.

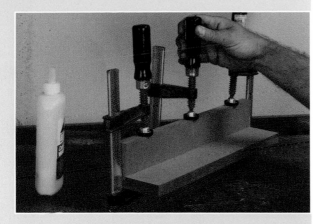

Clamp the parts to rip fence

To assemble the slip-on fence, start by butting the tall fence up against your rip fence. Then add the side and apply clamps as shown in the middle photo to draw the tall fence and side tightly against the rip fence. If you live in an area of the country where the humidity fluctuates quite a bit, consider inserting a piece of kraft paper between the side and the rip fence (as shown) before applying the clamps. This added clearance will help prevent the slip-on fence from binding as the humidity rises and the wood swells.

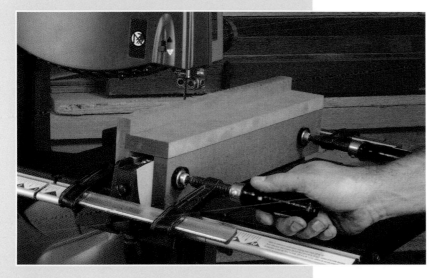

Screw the top to the side

All that's left is to drill pilot holes for the screws that fasten the top to the sides and drive in the screws as shown in the bottom photo. If you've built your fence from MDF (as shown here), make sure to drill full-length pilot holes down into the side as well to prevent the screws from splitting the side along its thickness when they're driven in.

Lumber-Cutting Fence

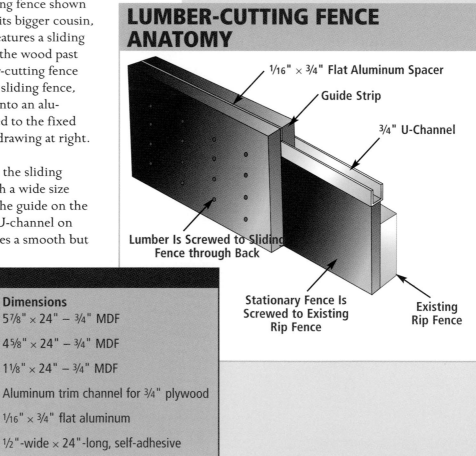

Much of the lumber that's being cut by local sawmills across the country is cut on a band saw mill. The advantages of band saw mills are many. But one of the biggest is that the thin blade that these saws use make smaller kerfs and waste much less wood than a mill fitted with a conventional saw blade. On many band saw mills, the blade is stationary and the wood log or billet is attached to a sliding carriage that moves the wood past the blade to produce uniformly thick pieces.

So why not use these same principles to produce your own lumber using your stationary band saw? That's exactly what we did when we designed the lumber-cutting fence shown in the top photo. Just like its bigger cousin, our lumber-cutting sled features a sliding fence or carriage to move the wood past the saw blade. The lumber-cutting fence consists of a fixed fence, a sliding fence, and a guide strip that fits into an aluminum U-channel attached to the fixed fence as illustrated in the drawing at right.

A series of holes drilled in the sliding fence make it easy to attach a wide size range of logs and billets. The guide on the sliding fence fits into the U-channel on the fixed fence and provides a smooth but precise sliding motion. The fixed fence attaches to your rip fence and can be easily moved to adjust the thickness of the cut. Although we designed our fence to fit the 14" Delta band saw, you can modify the dimensions as needed to fit your saw.

LUMBER-CUTTING FENCE ANATOMY

1/16" × 3/4" Flat Aluminum Spacer

Guide Strip

3/4" U-Channel

Lumber Is Screwed to Sliding Fence through Back

Stationary Fence Is Screwed to Existing Rip Fence

Existing Rip Fence

MATERIALS LIST

Part	Quantity	Dimensions
Sliding fence	1	5⅞" × 24" – ¾" MDF
Fixed fence	1	4⅝" × 24" – ¾" MDF
Guide strip	1	1⅛" × 24" – ¾" MDF
U-channel	1	Aluminum trim channel for ¾" plywood
Spacer	1	1/16" × ¾" flat aluminum
Glide strip	1	½"-wide × 24"-long, self-adhesive

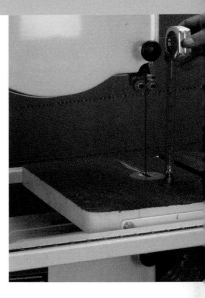

Determine height of fence

To build the lumber-cutting fence, you'll need to determine the height of the fence. Do this by first raising the upper guide assembly on your saw as far up as it will go. Then measure between the bottom of the guide assembly to the saw table as shown in the top right photo. Then subtract 1/8" from this measurement for clearance and cut a sliding fence to size.

Drill counterbored holes in U-channel

The U-channel that provides the smooth sliding action can be found in most hardware stores and home centers in the ready-cut metal rack. This channel is attached to the top of the fixed fence with a set of screws. Cut a piece of U-channel to match the length of the fixed and sliding fences, and then lay out and centerpunch a series of holes in the bottom of the channel. These holes should be evenly spaced, starting 1" in from the end and about every 4" to 6". Drill pilot holes first as shown in the middle photo, and then countersink each hole so the screw heads will sit just slightly below the surface of the U-channel.

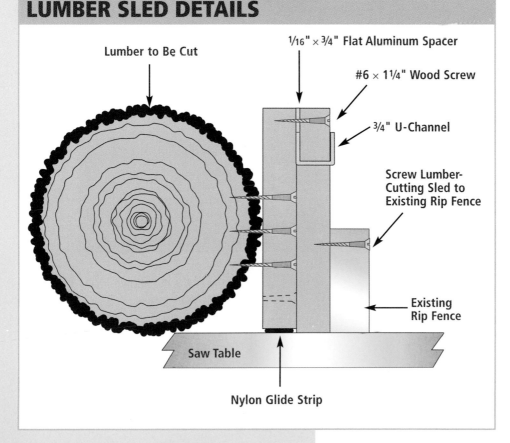

LUMBER SLED DETAILS

Lumber to Be Cut

1/16" × 3/4" Flat Aluminum Spacer

#6 × 1 1/4" Wood Screw

3/4" U-Channel

Screw Lumber-Cutting Sled to Existing Rip Fence

Existing Rip Fence

Saw Table

Nylon Glide Strip

Attach channel to the fixed fence

With all the holes in the U-channel drilled and countersunk, the channel can be attached to the top of the fixed base. (Note that the width of the fixed base is 1³/₈" narrower than the sliding base.) Position the U-channel on the fixed base so that one side of the channel is flush with the face of the fixed base, as illustrated in the drawing on the bottom of page 123. With the channel in place, drill pilot holes into the fixed base and then drive in screws as shown in the top photo.

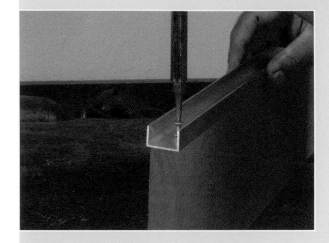

Attach guide strip and spacer to sliding fence

The mating part to the U-channel is the guide strip. It's attached to the top of the sliding fence. To compensate for the thickness of the side of the U-channel, a strip of ¹/₁₆" × ³/₄" flat aluminum is sandwiched between the guide strip and the sliding fence as illustrated in the drawing on page 123. Clamp the three pieces together so their top edges are flush, as shown in the middle photo. Then lay out and drill pilot holes through the guide strip and aluminum spacer strip and into the sliding fence; then drive in screws.

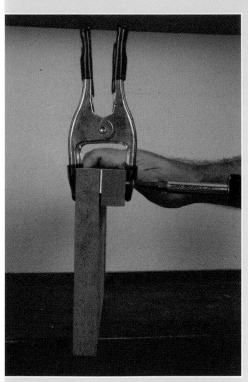

Add glide strip to bottom of sliding fence

Although the guide strip will do most of the work supporting the sliding fence and keep it sliding smoothly, the weight of the log or billet to be sawn can press the bottom of the sliding fence against the saw top. To prevent this from binding, we applied a ¹/₂"-wide strip of self-adhesive glide tape to the bottom of the sliding fence, as shown in the bottom photo.

Pegboard-drilling template

To make it easy to mount a variety of log and billet sizes to the sliding fence, we drilled a series of screw holes though the fence. The simplest way to lay out all these holes is to not lay them out. Instead, we used a technique we often employ when drilling holes for shelf pins—we used a piece of 1/4" pegboard as a drilling template. Cut a piece to fit under the guide strip and temporarily attach it to the inside face of the sliding fence with double-sided tape as shown in the top photo.

Mark hole locations on pegboard

We didn't want to drill holes at all the peg hole locations, as this would weaken the sliding fence. So we basically chose every other row. To make drilling less confusing, we marked each of the holes we wanted to drill through on the template with a marker as shown in the middle photo.

Drill marked holes in sliding fence

Now you can complete the lumber fence by drilling 1/4" holes through each of the marked locations on the pegboard as shown in the bottom photo. Remove the pegboard and countersink each of the holes you just drilled (as shown in the inset photo below) so that the heads of the screws that hold the log or billet to the sliding fence will sit below the surface and not interfere with the sliding motion.

■ USING THE LUMBER-CUTTING FENCE

The lumber-cutting fence is easy to use. The only challenge you'll have is getting your log or billet cut down to a size that'll fit onto the sliding fence. You can split the log with a sledgehammer and wood-splitting wedge. Or you can cut it down to size with a chain saw. Whichever method you choose, the log or billet needs to be narrower than the maximum cut of your saw and shouldn't be more and 12" or so longer than the sliding fence. Also, since much of this lumber will be green, make sure to completely clean the blade, saw table, and interior of your saw when you're done, as the dust and chips will be moisture-laden and can quickly cause metal parts to rust.

Attach fixed fence to rip fence. To use the lumber-cutting fence, start by attaching the fixed fence to your rip fence with screws. If your fence doesn't have holes drilled in it for this, lay out and drill three evenly spaced holes near the top edge of the fence. Then attach the sliding fence to the rip fence with stout screws (like a #10 or #12) as shown in the photo at right.

Attach lumber to sliding fence. With the fixed fence in place, the next step is to mount your log or billet to the sliding fence. Set the log or billet on your saw top and butt the outside face of the sliding fence up against it. Then drive a set of stout screws through the holes in the sliding fence into the log or billet as shown in the photo at right. Coarse-threaded screws grip best in wet wood; 1½" to 2" screws work well—drive them in about every 4" or so near both the top and bottom of the log or billet along its entire length.

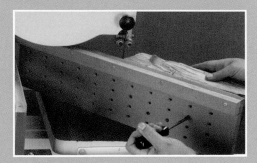

Adjust rip fence for desired cut. Now you can fit the two halves of the fence together and adjust the rip fence for the desired cut, as shown in the photo at left. Check the sliding action of the fence to make sure that it doesn't bind. If it does, you may need to reposition the log or billet on the sliding fence until there's no binding.

Cut the first piece. With the fence adjusted, you can make your first cut. Typically, this will be a cleanup cut to create a flat side for the face of your first board. Cutting lumber like this is virtually same as resawing, and so all the rules for resawing apply here: Use the widest blade your saw can handle, make sure to hook up dust collection, and use a steady but slow feed rate—you're removing a lot of wood here. When you've cleaned up one face, adjust your rip fence and cut the first piece as shown in the top photo.

Reset rip fence and cut again. Now it's just a matter of resetting your rip fence as you continue to cut boards off the log or billet. Make sure to stop well in advance of where the mounting screws that hold the log or billet to the sliding fence are located so you don't damage your saw blade. Also, if you built the shop-made table and fence described on pages 99–107, consider drilling a series of holes in the front edge of the table spaced 1" apart. Then if you drill a hole through the bracket on the fence aligned with these holes, you can insert a dowel or pin to "index" the fence to cut uniformly 1"-thick boards without having to reach for a tape measure or metal rule.

Sticker and stack. After you've cut all your boards, you'll need to let them dry. For this to occur properly, you'll need to do a couple of things. First, you should coat the ends of the boards to prevent moisture from wicking too fast out of the ends, causing the boards to check or split. Although you can purchase special sealing fluid for this, you'll get similar results by brushing on a coat of latex paint or yellow carpenter's glue. Then you'll need to stack the lumber so air can pass equally between the boards. Cut a set of "stickers" from dry close-grained wood (like maple or poplar) and insert these between the boards as shown in the bottom photo. When air-drying, the general rule is to allow one year per inch of thickness—but this varies widely depending on local climate.

6 Band Saw Maintenance

The average band saw is a pretty reliable machine. Odds are you'll spend more time maintaining it than repairing it. Typical maintenance includes: routine inspection, cleaning, and lubrication—as well as maintaining guide blocks, thrust bearings, and the tabletop, rip fence, and miter gauge. You'll also need to know how to maintain and modify blades, how to reduce vibration, and how to make common electrical repairs.

We cover all of that in this chapter, plus we'll show you how to add some common accessories like installing a height-attachment kit, installing an add-on fence, and how to replace your old guide blocks with roller and ceramic guides. Finally, we'll go over the more common problems—and their solutions—that you're likely to encounter when using your band saw.

Band saw maintenance is more than just keeping it clean and well lubricated. You also need to know how to tune up the saw, make simple repairs, and solve common problems.

Anatomy of a Band Saw

The blade of a band saw is a continuous toothed band that rides two or more wheels as illustrated in the drawing below. The wheels are covered with a rubber tire or band to grip the blade and hold it in position. The band also protects the blade's teeth. The lower wheel is the drive wheel and either is connected directly to the motor or is turned via pulleys and a V-belt. The upper wheel tilts forward and backward to "track" the blade on the wheels. Commonly, the tracking adjustment is a pair of locking knobs on the back of the saw case near the top wheel. The upper wheel is also connected to a mechanism that raises and lowers the wheel to increase or decrease the tension on the blade. Newer saws have a quick-release lever that makes changing blades easier.

The blade is supported near the workpiece by way of two guide assemblies: an upper and a lower. Each of these guide assemblies contains a thrust bearing and a pair of guide blocks (or bearings) that help keep the blade in place and support it during a cut so it doesn't deflect under cutting pressure. The lower guide assembly is fixed in place and the upper guide assembly, along with the blade guard, can be raised up or down as needed. The table of the saw can be tilted for bevel cuts and typically has a slot for a miter gauge. A kerf in the table allows you to remove and replace blades; a table pin keeps the halves of the table aligned.

BAND SAW ANATOMY

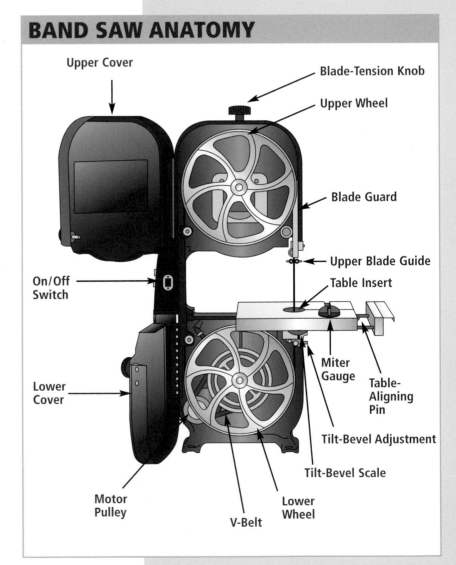

Upper Cover

Blade-Tension Knob

Upper Wheel

Blade Guard

Upper Blade Guide

On/Off Switch

Table Insert

Lower Cover

Miter Gauge

Table-Aligning Pin

Tilt-Bevel Adjustment

Tilt-Bevel Scale

Motor Pulley

Lower Wheel

V-Belt

Cleaning and Inspection

To keep a band saw running in peak condition, it's important to routinely clean the saw and regularly inspect it. How often you clean your band saw will depend on how frequently you use it. In some shops, a saw may need daily cleaning; in others, once a week or once a month is plenty. Every time you go to use your saw you should give it a quick "pre-flight" inspection to make sure everything is in good shape. A more thorough inspection, like the one described here, can be made less frequently.

the fresh lubricant will not have any effect. Also, not cleaning means dust will quickly contaminate the fresh lubricant. A shop vacuum fitted with a nozzle like the one shown in the bottom middle photo will make quick work of removing dust.

Remove blade and table

To give your band saw a thorough inspection, start by removing the blade as shown in the top middle photo and described on pages 38–39. Then loosen and remove the tilt knobs that secure the table to the saw and lift off the table (inset photo above).

Vacuum

With the blade and table off, you'll have full access to all the nooks and crannies where dust can build up inside the saw. If you're planning on lubricating your saw as described on pages 134–135, this is an essential first step, as parts must be cleaned before lubricating them; otherwise,

Brush the wheels

Even if your band saw has internal brushes to keep the wheels clean, odds are that you'll still experience some pitch and dust buildup on the wheel bands. An old toothbrush can be pressed into service to quickly scrub the wheels clean as shown in the photo above. Don't use a wire or brass brush for this, as it'll score the rubber surface of the band and could cause tracking problems. If pitch has built up and won't come off with the toothbrush, dip the brush in some mineral spirits or acetone and try again—this will usually do the trick.

Check wheel alignment

With the inside of the saw clean, the next step is to check the wheel alignment. For a band saw to run at peak performance, the wheels of the saw must be aligned, in the same plane. To check for this, press a long level or other known-accurate straightedge up against the wheels as shown in the top photo. Both the top and bottom rims of both wheels should touch the level or straightedge. There should be no gaps. If there are, see page 148 on how to correct this.

Thrust bearings

Now you can turn your attention to the upper and lower guide assemblies. Begin with the thrust bearings, removing any dust by blowing it off (as shown in the middle photo) or vacuuming it away. Slowly rotate each bearing to make sure it operates smoothly. Any catch or grinding indicates that the bearing is shot and needs replacing (see page 137 for more on this). Inspect the surface of the bearing that supports the blade for scoring or grooves. If you find any, replace the bearing.

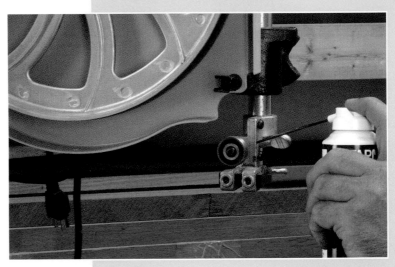

Guide blocks

Since the guide blocks on your saw frequently come in contact with the blade, they should be inspected often—at bare minimum, at least every time you change a blade. To do this, start by removing any built-up dust or pitch. An old toothbrush works well for this, as shown in the bottom photo. Remove each guide block and check the pad for scoring, dings, or dents. If you find any, you'll need to resurface the block as described on page 136.

Guide assemblies

Guide assemblies are more than just guide blocks and thrust bearings. The assemblies themselves—the actual holders and adjusting mechanisms of the guide blocks and bearings—also deserve regular cleaning and inspection. Blow the adjusting mechanisms clean with a blast of compressed air, and

wipe down any exposed surfaces with a clean cloth, like the upper guide post shown in the top photo.

Tabletop

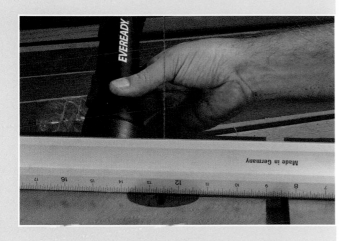

Just like the top of a table saw, the saw table on a band saw should be inspected routinely to make sure that it's flat. The simplest way to do this is to place a known-accurate straightedge on its edge on the top and shine a low-angle light behind the straightedge as shown in the middle photo. If you see light (as shown here), it indicates a low spot in the table. The low spot shown here is common—it's on both sides of the miter gauge slot. The area adjacent to the slot tends to rise up a bit, as the top is thinner at the slot and more likely to move. If you find low spots like this, take your tabletop to a local machine shop and have it ground flat.

Table tilt

The last thing to clean and inspect before reassembling the saw is the tilting mechanism. On many saws, including the one shown in the bottom photo, the curved faces of the tilting brackets are often painted or rough. Check for this by tracing your finger along the arc as shown. Any bumps or rough spots you find should be removed with a file or emery cloth. Some woodworkers prefer to strip off the paint in this area and sand it smooth before applying a lubricant; this is necessary only if the paint job is so rough and pitted that it prevents the tabletop from tilting smoothly in the holder.

Band Saw Lubrication

The best time to lubricate your saw is right after it has been cleaned and inspected as described on pages 131–133. At minimum, make sure to clean any part before you lubricate it; otherwise, sawdust will mix with the lubricant to form a thick goo that won't do the moving parts any good.

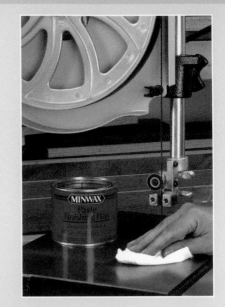

Tabletop

It's an old standard and it still works well—paste wax for a tabletop. Although there are newer spray-on lubricants and sealers (see page 141), paste wax does a good job of sealing your top and helping wood slide over it smoothly. Wipe on a generous coat with a clean cloth (as shown in the top photo), and then buff it to a dull sheen.

Wheel bearings

The bearings on most band saw wheels are sealed and do not—and cannot—accept lubrication. Check your owner's manual to see if the manufacturer of your saw recommends lubricating the wheel bearings and what type of lubricant they recommend. Some older saws utilize sleeve bearings in lieu of ball bearings; these require frequent lubrication with a light machine oil.

Tilt mechanism

The arced mating surfaces of the tilting mechanism—the brackets on the saw frame and the casting underneath the saw top—can benefit from the judicious application of a lubricant. White lithium grease in a stick form works well for this. Just glide the stick over the arced surfaces as shown in the bottom photo and wipe off any excess with a clean cloth. If your tilt mechanism employs rack-and-pinion gears to angle the table, first use an old toothbrush to fully remove any dirty residue from the teeth before applying a lubricant.

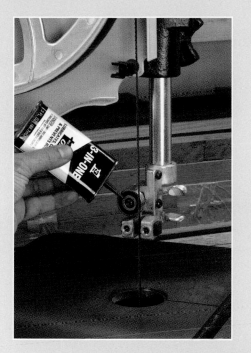

Thrust bearings

As with the saw's wheel bearings, most modern thrust bearings are sealed for life and cannot be lubricated. Bearings that are not sealed should be routinely lubricated with the lubricant that the manufacturer recommends. If you encounter sealed bearings that catch or grind, replace them as described on page 137.

Blade

Unlike most other saw blades, the blades of a band saw can be lubricated and will run smoother and longer if lubricated. What's important, though, is to use the correct lubricant. Some blade and accessory manufacturers sell a stick lubricant like that shown in the middle photo. This is basically a wax stick that is specially formulated to keep metal-, plastic-, and wood-cutting blades from clogging because of chips or pitch. The one sold here is made by the Olson Saw Company (www.olsonsaw.com).

Fence

Just like the tabletop, the surface of a rip fence should be routinely lubricated to help workpieces slide along smoothly. If your rip fence is made of cast iron, paste wax works well for this. Alternatively, any one of the numerous spray-on lubricants can be used. Just make sure to pick one that dries without leaving an oily residue (like the TopCote sealer shown in the bottom photo), as oil or silicone can bleed into your workpiece and will likely ruin any finish applied to the part.

Maintaining Guide Blocks

Since guide blocks constantly come in contact with a blade, they require frequent maintenance. How you maintain them will depend on what they're made of.

Loosen the screws

Regular maintenance of guide blocks means removing, inspecting, and surfacing them as needed. To remove your guide blocks, start by loosening the hardware that holds them in place. This can vary anywhere from a setscrew (like the one shown in the top photo) to a thumbscrew. Loosen these just enough to free the guide block.

Pull out each guide block

Grip each guide block and pull it out of the holder as shown in the middle photo. If the guide block won't come out easily, the surface may have been "mushroomed" by the blade and you'll need to file the lip of the mushroom off with a flat mill file to release the guide block. If the block still won't come out, remove the entire guide assembly from your saw (see pages 160–161 for more on this) and clamp the assembly in your bench vise. Use a pair of locking-grip pliers to grip the block and pull it out. Under no circumstance should you strike the guide block with a hammer, as you'll damage the guide assembly and will have to replace it.

Flatten ends

Once you've got the guide blocks out, inspect the ends for wear and resurface them as needed. Plastic and composite guide blocks (like those shown in the bottom photo) can be quickly resurfaced with sandpaper laid on a flat surface (like your tabletop). Steel blocks can be resurfaced on a grinder or with emery cloth placed on a flat reference surface.

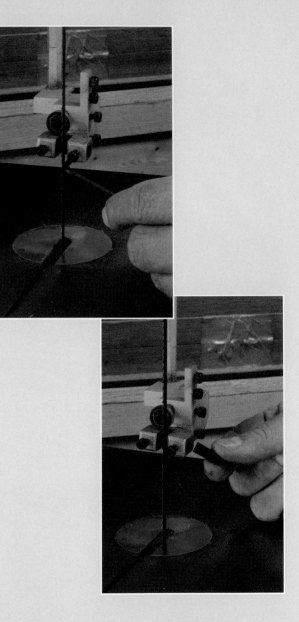

Maintaining Thrust Bearings

Just like the guide blocks on your saw, the thrust bearings come in frequent contact with the blade and also require regular maintenance. The two most common problems are: one or more bearings go bad, and the surface of the bearing gets scored or grooved by the blade. If you notice that either of your thrust bearings is scored, the bearing itself is likely shot because if the bearing were rotating as it should, odds are a groove couldn't be scored on its surface. If one bearing is bad, you're best off replacing both of them, as the other bearing will likely fail soon.

Loosen the screws
Thrust bearings are typically mounted onto the end of a metal post that's held in place in the guide assembly via a setscrew or thumbscrew. To remove your thrust bearings, first loosen these screws as shown in the top left photo.

Remove the unit
Next, slide the thrust bearing post out of its holder as shown in the bottom photo. In most cases, this will pull out easily. If it doesn't, remove the entire guide assembly and clamp it in your bench vise. Grip the

bearing post with locking-grip pliers and pull it out. You'll probably find that the side of the post where the setscrew comes in contact is dinged up from applying too much pressure to the screw. File off any ridges, and take it easy on the setscrew pressure in the future.

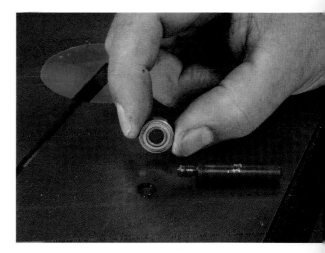

Remove the bearing
Bearings mount to the post in a variety of ways. On inexpensive versions, the bearing may just be pressed on and will require a bearing puller to remove the bearing. Often it's easier to simply order a new post / bearing assembly than to try to remove and replace the bearing. The bearings on better-quality saws are attached to the post via a screw like the one shown in the right middle photo. That's because the manufacturer realizes that bearings eventually wear out and need replacing. Make sure to order an exact replacement from the saw manufacturer. To install the new bearing, insert the post in the guide assembly and adjust its position as needed before locking it in place with the setscrew.

Wooden Guide Blocks

Guide blocks made from wood have a couple of advantages over steel and composite guide blocks. Unlike steel blocks, wood blocks can never hurt your blade when the teeth inadvertently come in contact with the blocks. Since you can make wood guide blocks out of scraps lying around the shop, they're basically free. They're also especially useful when you've got a narrow blade mounted on your saw—those narrower than 1/4". With a narrow blade, there's less body for the guide blocks to support. The beauty of wood blocks is that you can position them to wrap around the blade and fully support it without worry of dulling the teeth. When the ends do get scored, they're easy to flatten with sandpaper—no grinder needed.

Cut a strip to size

Wood guide blocks can be cut from most hardwoods, but you'll find that close-grained woods like hard maple tend to work the best, as they hold up well over time. To make wooden guide blocks, start by cutting a strip of wood to size to match the height and width of your existing blocks. The blocks we're cutting here are for a Delta 14" saw, so they're roughly 1/2" × 1/2". To cut a small strip like this safely on the table saw, make sure the strip ends up on the waste side of the blade as you make your final pass, as shown in the top photo.

Trim blocks to length

Once you've cut a strip or two, the next step is to trim the blocks to length. If you do this on the table saw, make sure to use a zero-clearance insert to prevent the blocks from falling into the opening in the insert. To hold the small strip safely, we clamped it to the miter gauge fence as shown in the middle photo. Measure the existing guide blocks and cut wood ones to match this length (there's usually no harm is cutting them a bit longer, as long as your holder will accept the additional length).

Sand the ends smooth

After you've cut all the blocks to length, it's a good idea to sand the ends smooth. Do this by placing a piece of sandpaper on a known-flat surface and then gently rub the end of the block back and forth on the sandpaper until the end is smooth, as shown in the bottom photo. Do this to both ends of each block so you can simply turn the block around if one end gets scored.

Spray ends with DriCote

Although it's not absolutely necessary, we've found that the guide blocks will perform best if the ends are sprayed with a lubricant such as DriCote, as shown in the top photo. Spray a light coat on both ends and allow them to dry before installing them in your saw. This lubricant holds up well to friction and will help prevent the ends of the guide blocks from burning.

Install the guide blocks

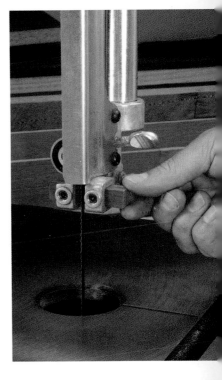

Once the lubricant is dried, you can install the guide blocks as you would any guide block, as shown in the middle photo. If they don't slide in easily, just sand them until they fit. Because they're wood, you'll want to take it easy on the setscrew pressure, as it's easy to crush the wood fibers. All you want to do is apply enough pressure to keep each block in place.

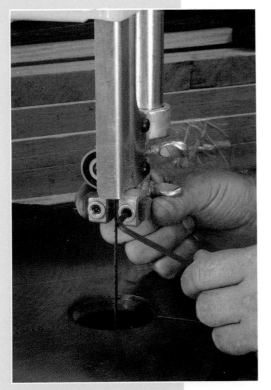

Adjust the guide blocks

Unlike other guide blocks, wood guide blocks can be pressed right up against the blade. An easy way to adjust these is to first press one block into the blade until it just makes contact. Then slide the other one over, taking care not to make the blade deflect. Now you can lock them in place by tightening the setscrews as shown in the bottom photo. Alternatively, you can use the standard gap (the thickness of a dollar bill) between the blade and the blocks.

Maintaining the Tabletop

Since every cut you make on a band saw involves sliding a workpiece across the top, it's important to keep the saw top maintained. In addition to helping workpieces slide smoothly, a properly maintained top will help ensure accurate cuts. Additionally, by sealing the top, you'll keep it rust-free.

Cleaning

Whenever you apply a sealer to the top to prevent rust and help workpieces glide, you should start by cleaning the top with a clean cloth dipped in solvent, such as the acetone shown in the top photo. This will remove any old sealant or other impurities on the saw top. Always check your solvent in an inconspicuous place to make sure it won't damage the top.

Smoothing

Once the top has been cleaned, it's good practice to follow this with an abrasive pad. Rub a pad across the entire surface of the saw top (as shown in the middle photo) to abrade away any rust or other minor surface imperfections.

Flattening

Occasionally, you'll come across heavy rust spots or other buildups that won't come off with the abrasive pad. In cases like this, you'll need to step up to a more aggressive abrasive. Emery cloth or silicon-carbide sandpaper wrapped around a scrap block or sanding block will do a good job of leveling most buildups and removing heavy rust; see the bottom photo. Start with a coarse grit (such as 100) and work up to around 320-grit to remove the scratches on the top that the prior grit left. Another product that's useful is rubber-bonded abrasive blocks sold under the Sandflex brand name (available at www.woodcraft.com). They come in fine, medium, and coarse grits and do a great job of removing rust from saw tops.

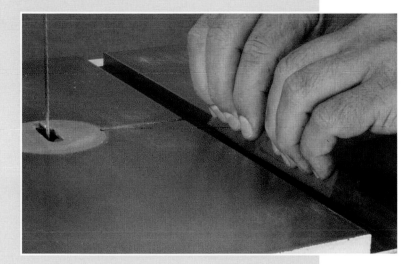

Miter gauge slot

Although the top edges of most miter gauge slots in saw tops are chamfered slightly, you'll often find that there are nibs or projections on the edges of a new saw. With this in mind, consider running the flat side of a small mill file over the edges of the chamfer to knock off any nasty bits, as shown in the top photo. Don't get carried away here. You don't want to remove any metal from the sides of the slots, because this can cause excessive side-to-side play in the miter gauge. If this does occur, see page 144 for some simple fixes.

Table insert opening

Although you don't reach into the opening in the saw top of a band saw like you do to change blades on a table saw, there will be times when you need to do this—as when adjusting the lower guide assembly from above. After you've lifted out the table insert, you may find that the metal edges inside the opening are cast, not machined, and can be rough and jagged. Grab a small round file and file the edges smooth all the way around the opening, as shown in the middle photo.

Lubricating

There are a number of excellent saw top sealers available that will seal your freshly cleaned, de-rusted and smoothed top. Most of these also leave a dry lubricant on the surface that promotes smooth cuts by helping workpieces glide effortlessly on the saw top. The two that we've had the most luck with are TopCote and Boeshield T-9. Both are simply sprayed on the top; see the bottom photo. Note: Before you spray, thoroughly vacuum your saw top to remove any dirt, dust, or leftover sanding grit—you don't want to seal this into the top. After the spray dries, buff off the film with a clean cloth as shown in the bottom inset photo.

Adjusting the table for square

With the top sealed and lubricated, you can turn your attention to a couple of adjustments. The first thing to do is check to make sure your tabletop is perpendicular to your saw blade. Do not rely on your tilt-angle indicator for this. Instead, use a small try square or combination square. Raise your upper guide assembly up as far as it will go, and then butt your square up against the blade as shown in the top photo. If there's a gap, loosen the table-tilt knobs and adjust the top until there is no gap between the blade and the square. If your band saw has an adjustable stop for 0 degrees, consult your owner's manual on how to adjust it—the stop is usually a bolt and jam nut that thread into the frame and make contact with the underside of the saw top. Adjustment usually involves loosening the jam nut and adjusting the bolt as needed before retightening the jam nut.

Adjusting the tilt-angle pointer

Once you've got your table adjusted so that it's perpendicular to the blade, take the time to adjust the tilt-angle pointer under the saw top (if it's adjustable). Generally, the indicator is held in place with a screw and a lock washer. Just loosen the screw and adjust the pointer to point to zero, as shown in the middle photo. Then tighten the screw.

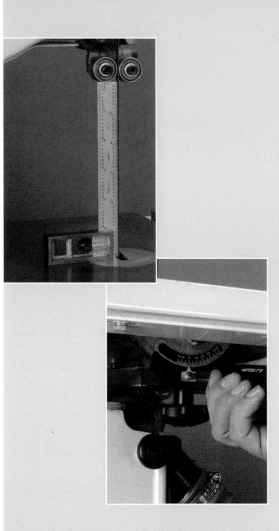

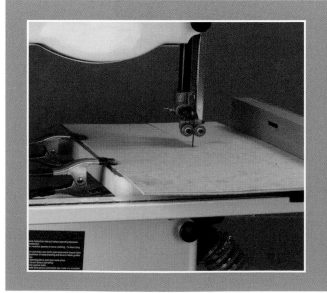

ZERO-CLEARANCE TOP

Occasionally you'll find the need to cut small or delicate parts that may be in danger of falling into the opening in the table insert. In cases like this, consider using a zero-clearance top to prevent this from happening. This top is nothing more than a scrap of 1/8" or 1/4" plywood that's clamped to the saw top. To make your own zero-clearance top, simply push the plywood into the blade and stop at the midway point as shown in the photo at left. Turn off your saw and clamp the plywood top in place. Since the plywood wraps around the blade, there's no gap for parts to fall into.

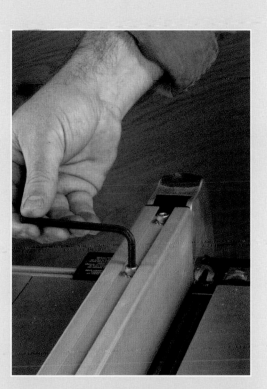

Maintaining the Fence

An improperly aligned rip fence can lead to inaccurate cuts. Fortunately, it's easy to both check and align most band saw rip fences.

Checking the alignment

When a rip fence is properly aligned, its sides are perpendicular to the saw top. Although you may not notice a misaligned fence when cutting thin stock, it'll be more obvious with thicker stock, and particularly when you cut tenons on the ends of boards. To check alignment, just butt a try square up against the fence as shown in the top right photo. There should be no gap between the square and the fence or the saw top. If there is, check your owner's manual for adjustment procedure. In most cases you'll have to shim the fence to bring it into alignment.

Adjusting the fence

If your rip fence is out of alignment or you want to angle it to compensate for drift (see page 51), start by loosening the rip fence mounting bolts to friction-tight, as shown in the top left photo. There are almost always two of these, and they may be bolts or machine screws with hex heads, slotted heads, or heads that accept an Allen wrench. Take care here to loosen them only enough to adjust the fence with a dead-blow hammer; see below.

With the rip fence bolts loosened to friction-tight, tap the end of the fence with a soft-faced or dead-blow hammer on the side that you want to angle it away from, as shown in the bottom photo. Tap lightly here and then check the alignment. If it's good, tighten the bolts and check one more time; tightening the bolts can often rack the fence out of alignment. If it's not aligned, tap again and repeat as necessary until it comes into alignment. Then retighten the bolts to lock the newly aligned or angled fence in place.

Maintaining a Miter Gauge

Besides the rip fence, the miter gauge is the second-most-used guide for making cuts on the band saw. That's why it's important to make sure it's aligned; see below. But being aligned does not guarantee accurate crosscuts—the miter gauge must slide smoothly back and forth in the slots with little or no play. Just a tiny bit of play here can cause a 1- to 4-degree error in the end angle of a board, depending on its width. If your miter gauge does exhibit any side-to-side play, remove this play first before checking alignment; see the sidebar below.

Alignment

A quick way to check miter gauge alignment is to use a try square. Butt the handle of a square up against the head of the miter gauge and slide it over until the blade butts up against the saw blade, as shown in the inset photo at left. Loosen the miter gauge handle to friction-tight, and adjust the position of the miter gauge head until the blade of the try square butts squarely up against the saw blade. Tighten the miter gauge handle and adjust the 90-degree stop if necessary.

REMOVING PLAY

Dimples. One way to remove side-to-side play on a miter gauge is to dimple the miter gauge bar, as shown in the top photo below. What dimpling does is create tiny raised crater-shaped ridges in the side of the bar. Dimples can be made with a centerpunch and a hammer (or with an automatic punch, as shown here). The harder you strike the punch, the more you raise the sides of the dimple. Start by striking a series of small dimples in the side of the bar. Work only where you know there's excessive play. Slip the miter gauge in the slot and check for play. What you're after here is a trade-off between no play and smooth movement. Increase the size of the dimples if necessary to remove play, or try dimpling the other side. If the bar gets too tight in the slot, knock the high points off the dimples with a block of wood wrapped in emery cloth.

Metal tape. A second way to remove excessive play is to apply metal foil tape to one or both sides of the miter gauge bar, as shown in the bottom photo. Metal foil tape can be found in the heating and cooling aisle in most home centers and hardware stores. It's used to seal the joints between connecting metal ducting. Because it's metal, it will hold up well to the wear and tear. Cut a strip to width, peel off the backing, and apply it to the side of the bar. If necessary, apply a strip or two to the opposite side until the side-to-side play is gone.

Reducing Vibration

Excess vibration is often the culprit behind inaccurate cuts. If possible, it's usually worth the effort to bolt your band saw to the floor if the legs or cabinet are designed for this (and if you don't mind drilling holes in your floor). Alternatively, you can dampen vibration by inserting rubber anti-vibration pads under the feet; these are sold in sheets by most mail-order woodworking catalogs. Another simple way to dampen vibration is to insert a hockey puck—yes, that's right, a hockey puck—under each leg. They're inexpensive and do a great job.

Tighten base/stand

Saw vibration can be caused by a base or leg assembly that's not rigid. That's why it's a good idea to periodically check and tighten any assembly bolts, as shown in the top photo. The ironic thing is that vibration is what usually causes the bolts to work loose in the first place. You should check your base once a month, after completing a large project where you worked the saw hard, and anytime you feel that the saw is vibrating excessively. If you're using a mobile base, it's especially important to check these bolts regularly, since moving a saw about can also cause assembly bolts to loosen.

Weigh down stand

Weight can be used to dampen vibration. The heavier your saw and stand are, the more likely they'll be able to reduce vibration. Consider adding weight to your stand in the form of sand or bricks, as shown in

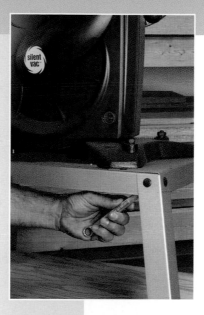

the middle photo. Bricks make less of a mess, but are not as heavy as sand. Sand-filled tubes are popular, as these can be draped over legs and stand shelves to increase the weight.

Align pulleys

If your saw is belt-driven, the motor connects to the saw arbor via a V-belt and a set of pulleys. For the saw to run smoothly, the two pulleys must be in line. Not only does this help reduce vibration, but it also prevents excessive wear and tear on the V-belt. To check alignment, slip a long straightedge into the cabinet so the straightedge is touching both edges of the saw arbor pulley as it spans the pulley. If the pulleys are aligned, the other end of the straightedge will contact both rims of the motor pulley as shown in the bottom photo. If the pulleys are out of alignment, there are a couple of ways you can adjust them back into alignment. One way is to loosen the setscrew that locks the motor pulley onto the motor shaft. Then slide the pulley in or out on the motor shaft until they are aligned. If there's not enough movement to bring them into alignment, try loosening the motor-mounting bolts and shifting the motor in or out as needed.

Maintaining Blades

Band saw blades require regular maintenance. Although carbide-tipped blades require much less frequent sharpening than high-speed steel (HSS) blades, both types will cut truer and last longer if stored properly and kept clean.

Cleaning blades

With day-to-day use, band saw blades will pick up pitch and gum from the woods you cut. If you cut a lot of soft-woods, the blades can pick up a lot of resin as well. Any of these build-ups on your saw blades will decrease the cutting efficiency of the blades and also tend to cause burning and ragged cuts. To promote blade cleaning, consider making a blade-cleaning kit consisting of an old tooth-brush, rubber gloves, and a can of pitch and gum remover. Keep a couple of old newspapers on hand as well to protect surrounding work surfaces. To clean a blade, put on a pair of rubber gloves and place the blade on the newspapers. Spray on a coat of pitch and gum remover and wait the rec-ommended time. After it has set, scrub the teeth with an old

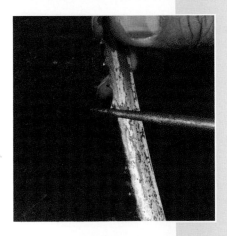

toothbrush or brass brush to remove stubborn deposits, as shown in the top photo. Wipe off any excess with the clean cloth, flip the blade, and clean the other side.

Sharpening blades

Just like any other high-speed steel blade in your workshop (like a plane or hand-saw blade), an HSS saw blade can be sharpened with a slim taper file like the one shown in the middle photo. As there are so many teeth on a band saw blade, we advise that you have this done profes-sionally because if you don't sharpen every tooth identically and set each alternate tooth perfectly, the blade will not run true. It can pull to one side or, if one or more teeth protrude even slightly, they'll do all the cutting and dull quickly, leaving a jagged cut. Touch-up sharpen-ing can be done by pressing a file against the tooth so it aligns with the bevel. Then take one or two passes with the file to create a fresh edge.

Storing blades

The number one thing you can do to increase the life of your saw blades is to store them properly when they're not being used. Proper storage includes replacing a blade in its original packaging, as shown in the bottom photo, or placing sheets of posterboard or cardboard between the blades, as shown in the inset photo above. Both of these methods keep the teeth from coming in contact with metal. The worst thing you can do is allow blades to lie on top of one another or hang them on a wall. When teeth touch, they dull (if high-speed steel) or fracture or chip (if carbide-tipped).

Modifying Blades

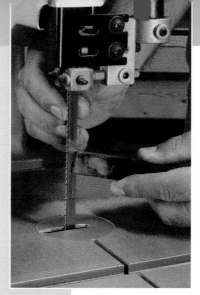

One of the nice things about band saw blades is that they're easy to modify if need be. There are two basic modifications you can do to a blade: clean up the weld, and hone the back and sides of a blade to enable you to make tighter-radius turns.

The weld

Band saw blades are made by cutting a band to length and then welding the ends together. Occasionally, you'll come across a blade where the

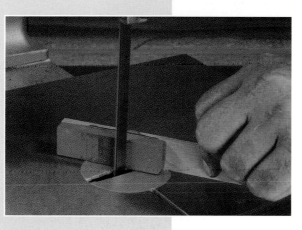

weld isn't as smooth as it should be. If returning the blade isn't an option, you can often clean up the weld yourself by running the flat portion of a small diamond hone over the weld (with the power off) as shown in the top photo.

Shaping the back for tighter-radius curves

The other blade modification you can do is useful if you're planning on cutting a tight radius. The idea is simple: If you round over the back corners of the saw blade, you can make tighter turns, as illustrated in the bottom left drawing.

Honing is easy to do. One way to do this is to place a small whetstone on edge behind the saw blade and turn on the saw. Make sure the edge of the whetstone is flat on the tabletop, or you can end up grinding the back edges at a taper. Press the whetstone gently up against the back corners of the blade to round them over. A safer alternative is to epoxy the whetstone onto a scrap of wood to create a sharpening paddle, as shown in the bottom photo. Use the paddle as you would the whetstone described above.

HONING THE BACK CORNERS

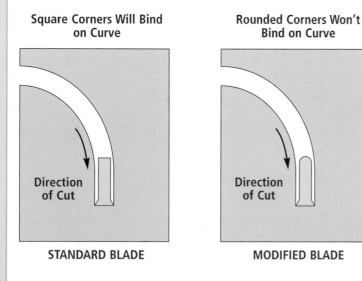

Square Corners Will Bind on Curve

Direction of Cut

STANDARD BLADE

Rounded Corners Won't Bind on Curve

Direction of Cut

MODIFIED BLADE

Wheel Repairs

If you've checked your band saw wheels to find out whether they're aligned and in the same plane (as described on page 132) and found that they are not aligned, you'll have to shim one of the wheels to bring them into alignment.

Remove the wheel

To shim a wheel, begin by removing the blade. Then use an adjustable wrench to loosen the wheel-mounting nut as shown in the inset photo at left. On some saws, you'll need to hold the wheel with one hand to keep it from spinning as you loosen the nut with the wrench as shown here. Other saws don't require this, as the nut threads onto a fixed bolt mounted to the frame of the saw. After you've removed the nut and any washers, you can pull the wheel off as shown in the top photo and then set it aside.

Install a shim

The thickness of the shim you'll need equals the gap between the rim of the band saw wheel and the level or straightedge that you used to check the alignment. You can find round washers in a wide variety of thicknesses at most hardware stores and home centers. Install the correct shim as shown in the middle right photo. Reinstall the wheel and check the alignment again and re-shim as needed.

REPLACING A WHEEL BAND

Quality band saw manufacturers sell replacement bands for their saws, as they know that these can get damaged and need to be replaced. Make sure to order an exact replacement band, and when it arrives, allow it to come to room temperature—a cold band will not stretch as much or as easily as a warm one.

Remove the old band and clean the wheel with mineral spirits or acetone. When dry, clamp a section of the band to the rim to keep it from sliding around and use a dowel to stretch the band around and onto the rim. Depending on the wheel and the band, this can be a simple or a challenging task. If the band is stubborn, enlist the aid of a helper to stretch the new band into place.

Electrical Repairs

The electrical system on most band saws is simple and straightforward. Power enters through the plug and continues up the electrical cord. On its way to the motor it passes through the on/off switch, which serves to control the flow of electricity. Any of these components can be replaced fairly easily using the manufacturer's replacement part.

Power switch

How difficult or easy it is to replace the power switch on your band saw will depend on the manufacturer and the type of switch you're replacing. Switches vary from simple toggle switches to more advanced magnetic switches.

To replace a switch, remove the cover plate and gently pull out the switch. Then note the wire colors and locations before removing the old switch. The most reliable way to replace any power switch is to disconnect one wire at a time and connect it to the corresponding terminal on the replacement switch, as shown in the top photo.

Cord

How readily you can replace an electrical cord depends mostly on the manufacturer. On some saws you have to crawl under the saw or flip it over to access the power connections. Other manufacturers offer detachable housings that provide relatively easy access. In any case, once the ends of the cord are in sight, make a note of wire colors, locations, and routing. Replace the cord by removing one wire at a time and installing the matching wire of the new cord.

REPLACING A MOTOR

The motors on band saws on open stands are the easiest to replace since the motor is fully exposed at the rear of the saw. Lift the motor to disconnect the drive belt, loosen and remove the motor-mounting bolts, and set aside. Reverse this to install the new motor. Motors on closed-base saws are the next easiest, as they are also belt-driven. The only challenge here is lack of elbow room inside the cabinet. Bench-top saws are the most difficult since you'll basically have to gut the insides of the saw to remove the direct-drive universal motor—and there's little room, as shown in the photos below. One tip that will help with reassembly is to thread screws back into the holes they came from as you remove parts. This helps keep track of the many parts. Also, have the exploded view diagram from your owner's manual on hand to serve as a visual reference.

Remove the lower wheel. To remove the motor of a bench-top band saw, first remove the blade. Then remove the wheel-mounting nut and pull off the wheel.

Remove the drive belt. Next, release the tension on the V-belt by loosening the adjustable lever on the motor mount. Then pull the V-belt off of the drive and wheel pulleys.

Remove the motor. With the V-belt off, you can now loosen and remove the motor-mounting hardware and lift off the motor. Reverse this procedure to install the new motor.

Installing a Height Attachment

If you're unsatisfied with the cutting capacity of your saw, check to see whether the manufacturer sells a height-attachment kit. A height-attachment kit extends the maximum cut capacity of your saw—that is, it allows you to cut thicker or wider (when resawing) stock.

Most height-attachment kits consist of a riser block that fits between the frame sections of the saw, a new blade guard, and a new post for your upper guide assembly (you'll also need to buy new longer blades). The kit we installed here is for a 14" Delta saw.

It's important to note that your band saw's original motor was designed for the standard cut capabilities. If you double the height capacity without increasing the motor horsepower, you'll likely be disappointed. You can't expect your old motor to be able to handle stock that's twice its capacity. If you'll only be cutting thicker and wider stock occasionally, this may not be necessary as long as you use a sharp blade and a very slow feed rate.

Remove the blade guard

The first step to installing a height attachment is to remove the blade and the table from the saw—it's also a good idea here to thoroughly vacuum out the inside of the saw. Then remove the existing blade guard that's next to the frame. Loosen the bolts at the top and bottom of the guard (as shown in the top photo) and lift off the guard and set it aside.

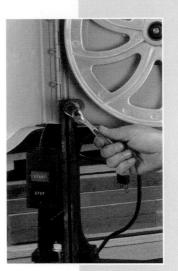

Loosen the frame hardware

Once the guard is removed, you can loosen the nut and bolt that secure the two halves of the frame together. Note that this is typically a very large, very stout nut and bolt, and you should measure these before you go to install the kit. For the Delta saw shown here, we needed a 1 3/16" open-end wrench for this (as shown in the middle photo)— not something the average woodworker usually has lying around the shop.

Remove the upper arm

On quality bands saws, each of the two frame sections are quite heavy, as they're often made of cast iron. Have a helper on hand to remove the upper arm. Start by threading off the nut you loosened in the prior step, and then lift the upper arm off the lower section as shown in the bottom photo and set it aside. Depending on your saw, you may first need to loosen or remove any hardware that secures electrical cables to the upper half of the frame in order to be able to set it aside.

Install the riser block

With the upper arm removed, take the time to clean the mating surfaces of the upper and lower arm to remove any built-up grease and dust. To align the riser block with the two halves of the saw, most manufacturers use round keys or roll pins that fit in holes drilled in the riser block and saw frame sections. Insert the roll pins in the bottom of the riser block, and align these pins with the holes in the lower frame as shown in the top photo. Press the riser block in place. If it doesn't slide in easily, try persuading it with a scrap of wood (to protect the edges of the riser block) and a rubber mallet.

Insert the roll pins

Now that the riser block is in place, you can insert the roll pins in the holes on top of the riser block as shown in the middle photo. In most cases, these will slip right into the holes. For stubborn pins, tap them in gently with a hammer, taking care to not mushroom the heads of the pins, or the upper arm won't fit over them.

Reinstall the upper arm

With the aid of a helper, lift the upper arm of the saw up and onto the lower arm, taking care to align it with the pins you just installed, as shown in the bottom photo. Generally, the weight of the upper arm will be sufficient to bring the mating surfaces together. If it's not, try rocking the arm gently back and forth until the surfaces mate.

Fasten upper to lower arm

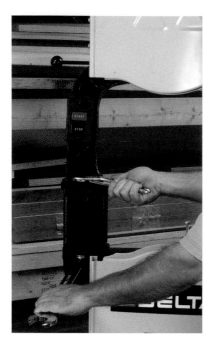

Have your helper hold the upper arm in place while you thread the new longer frame bolt through the holes in the upper arm, riser block, and lower arm. Add the washer and thread on the nut. Then use a pair of wrenches to fully tighten the nut onto the bolt as shown in the top photo.

Attach new blade guard

Since the saw's cutting capacity has been increased, you'll need to install the new longer blade guard that's included with the kit. It will likely use the same hardware used to hold the old guard in place. Thread the bolts through the ends of the guard and secure it to the frame with a socket or box wrench as shown in the middle photo.

Remove upper guide assembly

Increased cutting capacity also means that your existing upper guide assembly won't extend all the way down to the saw top. This means you'll need to install a longer guide post. To do this, start by removing the upper guide assembly from the guide post. In most cases, it's held in place with a setscrew in the rear of the assembly. Then loosen the upper guide assembly adjustment knob and slide out the short post as shown in the bottom photo.

Install the longer guide post

Now you're ready to install the longer upper guide post. Simply slip this into the upper guide post holder as shown in the top photo and tighten the upper guide adjustment knob to lock it in place.

Attach the new guard assembly

Most height-adjustment kits come with some form of new guard assembly. This may simply be an extension bar, although in the case of the Delta kit shown here, it consists of a two-piece assembly that is attached above the upper guide assembly in the back of the saw, as shown in the middle photo. Note that with some kits it may be necessary to modify the guard to fit an older version of the saw.

Adjust the guard assembly

If necessary, adjust the new guard assembly to fully cover the exposed blade. On the Delta kit shown here, the two sections of the guard slide against one another and are locked in place with a wing nut (as shown in the bottom photo) once the blade is covered. Now you can reinstall the saw top and install a new longer blade. In the case of the Delta saw shown here, you'll be moving from a standard blade length of $93^{1}/_{2}$" up to a blade that's 105" long. Adjust the upper and lower guides as described on pages 40–41 and enjoy your new increased cutting capacity.

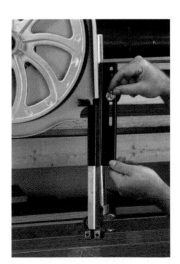

Installing an Add-On Fence

A rip fence is an essential accessory for your band saw. You'll need one to rip to width, to resaw, and to cut most joinery. If your band saw didn't come with one, and/or the manufacturer doesn't offer one, consider purchasing an add-on fence like the Kreg precision band saw fence (www.kregtool.com) that we installed on the Delta 14" band saw shown here. Most fence kits will fit a variety of saws.

Attach the front rail

All rip fences need at least one smooth, accurate surface to use as a reference. Since the castings on most saw tops are rough, the majority of rip fences slide back and forth on a rail or rails attached to the front and/or back edges of the saw top. The Kreg fence shown here uses a single front rail. The first step to installing an add-on fence is to install the rail or rails. Using the hardware supplied by the manufacturer, thread the bolts through the holes in the rail and into the threaded holes in the saw top edge as shown in the top photo. Leave these friction-tight since you need to adjust the rail before locking it in place; see below. Note that if the mounting holes pre-drilled in the rail don't align with your saw top holes, you can drill holes in the rail as needed; see the installation manual that came with your fence for specific instructions on locating and drilling these holes.

Align the rail

To prevent the rail from interfering with the miter gauge when it's used, you need to align the top of the rail with the bottom of the slot. An easy way to do this is to place a straightedge in the bottom of the miter gauge slot as shown in the middle photo and then raise the rail up so it sits just below the straightedge. Note that we also place a torpedo level on the rail to level it.

Tighten the rail-mounting bolts

When you've got the rail aligned so it doesn't interfere with the miter gauge slot and it's level, tighten one mounting bolt and then the other, as shown in the bottom photo. To keep the rail from shifting out of position as you do this, alternately snug up the bolts in small increments.

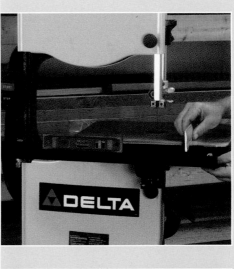

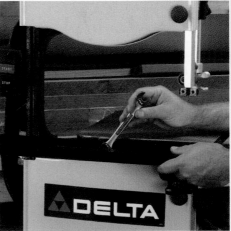

Assemble the clamping block

With the front rail in place, you can turn your attention to the rip fence. With most kits this will involve some assembly. With the Kreg fence, the first step is to assemble the clamping block. This block slides back and forth on the front rail and locks it in place at the desired location. Attach the adapter bracket onto the clamping block with the hardware provided, as shown in the top photo.

Attach the track

Now you can attach the fence or track to the adapter bracket with the hardware provided, as shown in the middle photo. With the Kreg system shown here, the heads of two bolts slip into a slot in the back of the track so you can slide the track back and forth as needed, as well as switch from high to low fence positions, as described on page 158. The body of the bolts slip into notches in the adapter bracket and are locked in place via a set of plastic knobs.

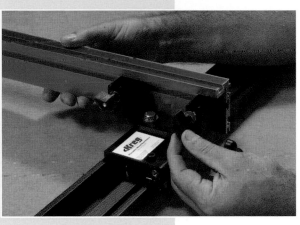

Test and adjust as needed

With the fence assembled, slip the clamping block onto the front rail and test the operation by sliding the fence back and forth on the rail. If it binds, locate the two nylon setscrews near the front edge of the clamping block, as shown in the bottom photo. Adjust these until they make contact with the mounting rail—this should alleviate any binding.

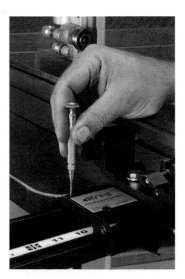

ATTACHING THE TAPE

Quality add-on fences will include a self-adhesive tape that attaches to the front rail so you can quickly and precisely position the rip fence. Since all saw tops and blade locations are different, you'll need to install the tape once the front rail has been attached.

Position the fence. To install the measuring tape, start by sliding the rip fence over until it just barely butts up against the saw blade, as shown in the top photo. Make sure that you don't cause the blade to deflect with the rip fence. Setting the fence next to the blade will define the zero mark on the measuring tape.

Scribe a reference mark. With the rip fence in place, the next step is to locate the zero point on the front rail. To do this, carefully extend the red indicator line on the lens down onto the front rail by drawing a line on the rail as shown in the middle photo. For added accuracy, use a small engineer's square to extend the line.

Install the tape. Now you can install the tape. Peel back a couple inches from the end of the tape and carefully align the zero mark on the tape with the line you just marked on the front rail. Press the tape in place and then slowly work out toward the end of the rail, peeling the tape as you go and pressing it in place as shown in the bottom photo.

Adjust the track

Once the tape is installed, the rip fence is almost ready to use. First, though, there are a couple of things to check. For cuts to be precise, especially when cutting thick or tall stock, it's imperative that the face of the rip fence be perpendicular to the saw top. To check for this, butt a small engineer's square up against the fence as shown in the top photo. A quality add-on fence will have an adjustment or adjustments so that you can tweak the fence as needed so there are no gaps between the fence, top, and square.

Check for drift

As with any fence, you'll need to check for blade drift. To do this, strike a line down the edge of a scrap of wood. Then turn on the saw and cut into the scrap, taking care to follow the line. Angle the scrap as needed to keep on track. Stop at the midway point as shown in the middle photo. Any angle equates to the drift or lead of the blade, and the fence will have to be adjusted to match this angle.

Adjusting for drift

To adjust the rip fence to compensate for blade drift, loosen the screws that secure the fence to the clamping blocks as shown in the bottom photo. Take care to loosen these to just friction-tight. Next, gently slide the fence over until it butts up against the angled scrap, angling the fence as needed. Then tighten the bolts you loosened previously. Remember that every time you change a blade, you'll need to check it for drift and will likely need to readjust the fence to match the new drift.

USING THE FENCE

Once you've adjusted your rip fence, it's ready to be used. There are a couple of unique features of the Kreg fence that are worth mentioning here. These include the precision measuring system and multi-position fence described below and the thoughtful accessories described on page 159.

Measuring system. One of the things we were impressed with on the Kreg add-on fence was the built-in measuring system that allows you to accurately and repeatably position the rip fence. Their measuring system consists of measuring tape and a hairline lens indicator fastened to the clamping block. As long as you follow their installation instructions, you can simply slide the fence over until the indicator reads the desired measurement (as shown in the top photo) and make the cut with confidence, knowing full well it'll be accurate.

Vertical for most cuts. Another feature that impressed us with the Kreg fence was its multi-position capability. This is possible because of the mounting system they used to secure the fence (or the track, as they refer to it) to the clamping block that locks the fence in place on the front rail. For standard use, the fence is installed on the clamping block vertically as shown in the middle photo. You can handle about 90% of your cuts with the fence in this position.

Horizontal for narrow cuts. What's nice with this system is that you can slide off the fence and install it in a horizontal mode, as shown in the bottom photo. The position is perfect for narrow cuts, where the fence would normally prevent you from lowering the upper guide assembly down far enough to cover the exposed blade. The horizontal fence position eliminates the interference caused by the fence by extending it out low on the table as shown.

Kreg Tool offers two well-thought-out accessories for their add-on rip fence: a fence micro-adjuster and a resaw attachment. The micro-adjuster lets you make even the tiniest of adjustments to the fence without worrying about it shifting out of place. The resaw attachment provides a single-point contact for resawing.

Adding the micro-adjuster. The micro-adjuster is easy to install. It consists of an adjustable block that threads into the side of the clamping block as shown in the top photo. The base of the block rests on the front rail and is locked in place via a plastic knob.

Using the micro-adjuster. To use the micro-adjuster, start by loosening its clamping knob and the locking knob on the clamping block of the rip fence. Then slide the fence roughly in position and lock the micro-adjuster to the front rail. Now you can turn the knurled brass knob of the micro-adjuster to move the rip fence in very small increments. When the rip fence is in its desired location, lock down its knob. If you need to readjust, loosen the rip fence knob, tweak the knurled knob, and retighten the rip fence knob as shown in the photo at right.

Adding the resaw guide. The resaw guide attaches to the front of the rip fence via a set of bolts and knurled brass knobs. The heads of the bolts pass through the attachment and fit into slots machined on the face of the rip fence. Just slide the attachment over until the high point or crown of the attachment is in line with the teeth of the saw blade. Then tighten down the knurled knobs.

Using the resaw guide. To use the resaw guide, adjust the rip fence over for the desired cut. Then strike a line along the length of your workpiece to match this width. Turn on the saw and push the workpiece into the blade, angling it as necessary to produce a uniformly thick cutoff as shown in the bottom photo.

Installing Roller Guides

A common problem with a band saw—a blade that doesn't run true—can be solved by replacing standard guide blocks with ball-bearing guides, like the those shown in the top left photo made by Carter Products (www.carterproducts.com). The roller guides we installed here are designed for a 14" Delta saw—Carter makes guides to fit most band saws.

Remove the upper guide assembly

To install a set of roller guides, first remove the old upper guide assembly. This is typically held in place with a setscrew in the back of the assembly. This screw fits into a groove in the column post. Loosen the setscrew and pull off the upper guide assembly as shown in the middle left photo.

Attach the guard bracket and guard

Since the old upper guide assembly you just removed also held the blade guard, you'll need to add a guard bracket and guard to the column post. Slip the guard bracket onto the post and tighten the setscrew friction-tight so you can still adjust its position, as shown in the bottom right photo. Then attach the guard to the bracket with the hardware provided, as shown in the inset photo at left.

Attach the new upper guide assembly

Now you can slip the new upper guide assembly over the bottom of the column and lock it in place with the setscrew provided, as shown in the top right photo. Once in place, slide the guard bracket down until it contacts the upper guide assembly, and fully tighten the setscrew.

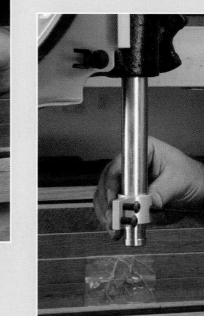

Remove the lower guide assembly

With the upper guide assembly in place, you can turn your attention to the lower guide assembly. To make installation easier, first remove the saw top and set it aside. Then loosen the screws that hold the lower assembly in place and remove it as shown in the top photo. Note that one of these mounting screws was so tight that we had to break it free with an impact screwdriver. This is quite common on older saws that have seen a lot of use—the constant vibration of the saw combined with rust can really freeze up a screw or bolt.

Attach the new lower guide assembly

Before you install the new lower guide assembly, take a moment to clean behind the bracket, and if your old screws needed persuasion to come out, apply a drop or two of machine oil to the threads of the mounting holes. Then install the new guide assembly as shown in the middle photo. Some guide kits provide new screws, others don't. The nice thing about the screws provided with the Carter kit is that they're hex-head and are tightened and loosened with an Allen wrench as shown. This type of screw or bolt is much easier to loosen, as it won't strip out like an ordinary screw.

Adjust the roller and thrust bearings

Once both guide assemblies are in place, attach the saw table and install a blade. Then adjust the guide bearings as you would a standard guide block, using a dollar bill to set the gap. On the Carter guides, the bearing rests on a cam that when turned with an Allen wrench (as shown in the bottom left photo) will pivot the bearing in and out for adjustment. Finally, adjust the thrust bearings (bottom inset photo).

Installing Ceramic Guides

One of the reasons that the band saws manufactured by Laguna Tools (www.lagunatools.com) are so terrific has much to do with their guide system. On their saws, they replace standard guide blocks with a unique ceramic guide block system. Each guide assembly has two sets of ceramic guide blocks to help prevent the blade from bowing or deflecting in use. And in place of thrust bearings, they use ceramic disks. The ceramic is so tough, odds are you'll never wear out a set of these guides. The folks at Laguna were deluged with requests from woodworkers who didn't own a Laguna saw but wanted a set of ceramic guides to fit their saw. So Laguna started manufacturing replacement guides for a wide variety of saws. The guides shown here are designed for a 14" Delta band saw. One thing to note here: These are quality guides and they're not inexpensive.

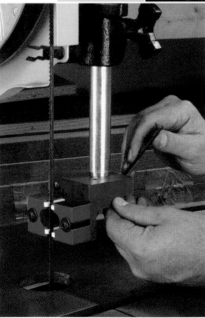

Remove the upper guide assembly

To install the Laguna ceramic guides, start by removing the old upper guide assembly. This is typically held in place with a setscrew in the back of the assembly. This screw fits into a groove in the column post. Loosen the setscrew and pull off the upper guide assembly, as shown in the top photo.

Attach the new upper guide assembly

At this point you can slip the new upper guide assembly over the bottom of the column and lock it in place with the setscrew provided, as shown in the middle photo.

Remove the lower guide assembly

Once the upper guide assembly is in place, you can start on the lower guide assembly. To make installation easier, first remove the saw top and set it aside. Then loosen the screws that hold the lower assembly in place and remove it as shown in the bottom photo.

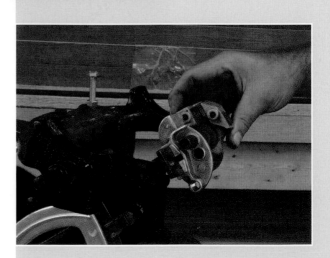

Attach the new lower guide assembly

It's a good idea to clean behind the old lower assembly bracket before you install the new bracket, as shown in the top photo. Some guide kits provide new screws, others don't. The Laguna guides shown here use the same screws that held the old guide assembly in place.

Adjust the ceramic guides

To adjust the ceramic guide blocks, first install a blade. Next, loosen the bolt in the sideways adjustment bracket and move the guide assembly until the blade is in the center of the back blade guide, and then tighten the bolt. Now loosen the clamp on the guide shaft and slide the guide assembly forward until the ceramic blocks are just behind the gullets of the teeth. Next, wrap a dollar bill around the blade and then gently bring the side blocks in until they touch the dollar bill before you tighten the adjustment bolts as shown in the bottom left photo.

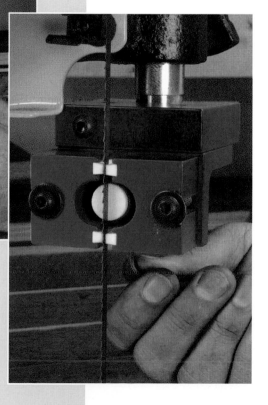

Adjust the back guide

The back guide block is adjusted much like a standard thrust bearing. Simply loosen the appropriate screw and slide the guide forward until it just barely touches the back of the blade before you tighten the screw as shown in the bottom photo.

■ TROUBLESHOOTING

As you use your band saw, odds are that you'll come across a variety of problems. In this section, we'll discuss the more common ones you'll encounter, including: wandering cut, angled cut, burning, ragged cut, workpiece jams, motor bogging down, and a barrel cut.

CUT WANDERS
A blade that frequently wanders off a cut line can be caused by a number of things: blade drift, insufficient tension, and lack of a guide.

Blade Drift
The most common cause of a wandering cut—where the blade tends to go off on its own, as shown in the photo above—is the result of blade lead or drift. This is caused by an uneven set of the teeth and is likely to be encountered with almost every band saw blade. The solution to this problem is to not fight the drift, but instead to go with it. There are two ways to do this. One way is to identify the drift as described on page 51 and then adjust your rip fence to match this angle. Second, you can use a single-point contact fence (like the one described on page 74) and angle the workpiece as needed to keep the blade on track.

Insufficient tension
Another reason a blade can wander during a cut is that it's not tensioned properly. A loosely tensioned blade can easily bow during a cut, especially if it encounters dense wood (like a knot). The solution is simple: Increase the tension. As a general rule of thumb, you'll want to tension a blade to the next higher width, as shown in the middle photo.

Use a guide
Finally, a wandering cut may be simply due to operator error—that is, you're not presenting the workpiece to the blade accurately. The easiest and most reliable way to get around this is to use some sort of guide, like a rip fence or miter gauge, as shown in the bottom photo.

■ TROUBLESHOOTING

ANGLED CUT

An angled cut, where the cut line is not parallel to the face of the workpiece, is a fairly common problem, particularly when resawing. The reason it's so prevalent when resawing is you're generally cutting through wider stock, so even a small angle error can show up as rather pronounced, like the board shown in the top photo.

Table not square

The first thing to check if your saw is producing angled cuts is the saw top. Don't rely on the angle indicator below the table—these are notoriously inaccurate. Raise your upper guide assembly up as far as it will go and then butt your square up against the blade as shown in the bottom photo. If there's a gap, loosen the table-tilt knobs and adjust the top until there is no gap between the blade and the square. If your band saw has an adjustable stop for 0 degrees, consult your owner's manual on how to adjust it—the stop is usually a bolt and jam nut that thread into the frame and make contact with the underside of the saw top. Adjustment usually involves loosening the jam nut and adjusting the bolt as needed before retightening the jam nut.

Upper and lower guides not aligned

If your table is square and you're still getting angled cuts, the next thing to do is to check to make sure your upper and lower guide assemblies are aligned. To do this, remove the guide blocks from both assemblies and then remove the table. Now place a straightedge between the assemblies flat against the inside face of the guide block holder. Press a torpedo level against the straightedge. If it's plumb, the assemblies are aligned. If they're not, they'll angle the blade as illustrated in the drawing below. This is also bad for the blade, as it puts it under excessive pressure that it's not designed to handle. Consult your owner's manual for the recommended adjustment procedure to correct this problem.

GUIDE-BLOCK ALIGNMENT

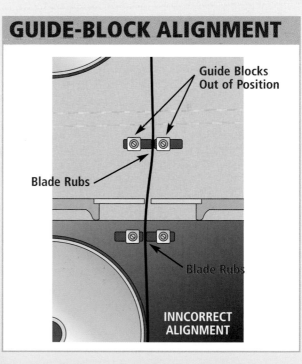

Guide Blocks Out of Position

Blade Rubs

Blade Rubs

INNCORRECT ALIGNMENT

SOMETIMES IT'S THE WOOD

Finally, an angled cut can be caused by the workpiece. If the faces aren't parallel and the edges aren't perpendicular, the workpiece may be angled as you present it to the blade. If this is a common occurrence in your shop, check your workpieces. If they're not square, inspect the tools you use to square them. A small tilt of a jointer's fence or a tilt of a table saw's rip fence is all it takes sometimes.

■ TROUBLESHOOTING

BURNING

Burning is a common problem on the band saw, especially with beginners who haven't developed proper technique and haven't learned the radius-turning rules.

Feed rate too slow

One reason wood burns or scorches (like the workpiece in the top left photo) is because too slow of a feed rate is used—this is particularly pronounced in cherry, which has a well-deserved reputation for burning. When your feed rate is too slow, the blade spends too little time cutting and more time simply rubbing up against the sides of the kerf. The friction that results from the rubbing can easily generate sufficient heat to burn the wood. The solution is to increase your feed rate. How do you find the correct rate? Experiment. Too slow, the wood burns. Too fast, and you'll hear the motor bogging down. What you want is a feed rate in between these two.

Too tight a radius

Another reason wood burns while being cut on the band saw is that you're trying to cut too tight of a radius for the width of the blade that's installed (see page 54 for radius rules). The solution is either to cut a wider radius or switch to a narrower blade. Remember to keep the workpiece moving on tight curves. If you stop, the resulting friction can create enough heat to burn.

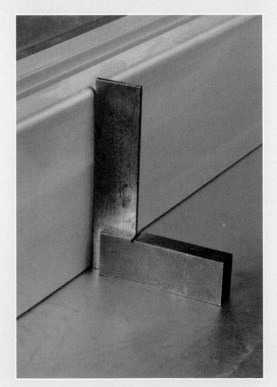

Improper alignment

If the rip fence is out of alignment and angles in toward the saw blade, it'll pinch the workpiece between the fence and the blade, and the wood will burn. You can prevent this from happening by checking the fence alignment with an engineer's square. Just butt it up against the fence as shown in the bottom photo. Adjust or shim as necessary to remove any gaps found between the fence, blade, and/or saw top.

CASE-HARDENING

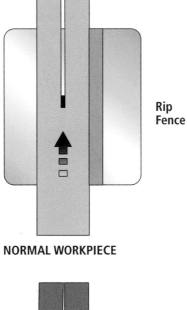

NORMAL WORKPIECE

Rip
Fence

■ TROUBLESHOOTING

RAGGED CUT

There are a couple of reasons why you may encounter a ragged or rough surface (like the one shown in the top right photo) when cutting on the band saw.

Dull or dirty blade

If you're experiencing ragged cuts on woods that aren't finicky (like most straight-grained domestic hardwoods and softwoods), the first thing to look at is your blade. A dull or dirty blade will not cut cleanly. See page 146 for information on cleaning (as shown in the middle photo) and sharpening your blades. Additionally, a ragged cut can be caused by misaligned guide assemblies, as described on page 165. Too fast a feed rate can also be the culprit.

WORKPIECE JAMS

Occasionally you'll encounter a jam when making a cut—this is most often caused by the wood itself.

Case-hardening

Case-hardening is caused by improper drying and cannot be detected without cutting into a board. The problem arises because of a difference in moisture between the surface and the core of the wood. When case-hardened wood is cut, internal stresses force the kerf apart—or more commonly together—like the board shown in the drawing at left. When the kerf closes, it pinches the blade and can even stop it. Unfortunately, there is no fix for this problem. Just turn off your saw and pitch the wood in the trash pile or burn bin. A reputable lumberyard will replace the wood or refund your money.

PREVENTING PINCHING WITH WEDGES

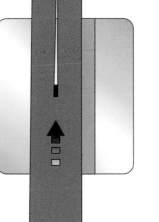

If, as you make a cut, you notice that the kerf is starting to close, you may be able to salvage the wood. If the wood is just a bit case-hardened (as described above), stop the saw and insert a wedge or two into the kerf as shown in the photo at left. Drive the wedge in far enough to open the kerf back up. Then continue your cut, stopping as needed to insert more wedges.

■ TROUBLESHOOTING

MOTOR BOGS DOWN

So you're happily cutting wood in your shop and sud-
denly the saw bogs down. You can hear it because the
tone of the saw motor drops, and you feel it because
it's harder to feed the wood into the saw. What's
happening here is that friction (from one source or
another) is loading down the saw blade and motor.
When this occurs, stop and turn off the saw. Allow
the blade to come to a complete stop and then
remove the workpiece. If you continue cutting, the
motor will draw more power and can blow a fuse or
circuit breaker. If by chance you have a high-amperage
line running to the saw (say, a 30-amp line for a motor
that requires 20 amps), you can overheat the motor and
damage it.

Motor underpowered

A saw that bogs down may be telling you that you're trying
to bite off more than it can chew. Bench-top saws typically
have small universal motors (top photo), and these just
can't handle some of the more stout cuts that a larger saw
can handle. If you experience this problem on a regular
basis, it's time to upgrade to a stronger motor or larger saw.

Wood is too tough

Sometimes a motor bogs down because you're cutting a
wood that it can't handle, like the white oak shown in the
middle photo. Sure the saw can handle thinner stock in
this species, but if you start trying to cut 4" oak, the saw
will let you know it can't handle it. Your only solutions here are to
upgrade to a more powerful motor, change woods, or have a friend with a
beefier saw cut it for you.

Wood is pinching blade

Wood can sometimes slow down a motor. A board that's case-hardened
(as explained on page 167) can close up a kerf so hard it'll stop a motor
(bottom photo). It's also easy to bog down a motor either by using a dull
blade or by trying to feed the wood too quickly into the blade. This is
particularly noticeable on bench-top saws with universal motors. Try
reducing your feed rate and make sure to use a clean, sharp blade.

■ TROUBLESHOOTING

Belt/pulley out of alignment

Finally, if you have a belt-driven band saw and the motor pulley and saw pulley are not aligned (top photo), the motor can easily bog down during a cut. That's because the motor expends energy overcoming the misalignment. This is particularly noticeable when you make a heavy cut, as when resawing or cutting thick stock. The solution is to check and align your pulleys as described on page 145.

BARREL CUT

Anyone that's ever resawn a board has likely encountered a barrel cut like the one shown in the photo at right. There are two common causes of this, both easily remedied.

Wrong and/or dull blade

One common cause of barreling is that you're using the wrong blade and/or it's dull, like the one shown in the middle left photo. Whenever you resaw, you remove a tremendous amount of wood. A dull blade just can't handle this and will flex trying to keep up with your intended feed rate. A wrong blade—usually too narrow or too many teeth per inch—will also flex under a heavy cut. In either case, install a stout resaw blade—preferably the widest your saw can handle, and make sure it's clean and sharp.

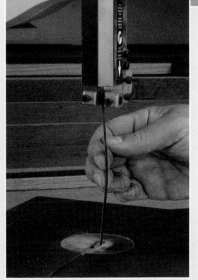

Not enough tension

The other common cause of barreling is that the blade is insufficiently tensioned. Combine a heavy cut with an under-tensioned blade, and flex will occur. The solution is to simply increase the blade tension. In most cases, you should increase the tension up to the next widest blade. For example, a 3/4" resaw blade should be tensioned as if it were a 1" blade. When it's properly tensioned, you should not be able to flex the blade easily from side to side as is shown in the bottom photo.

7 Band Saw Projects

Although the band saw is generally used in conjunction with other power tools to build a project, some projects can be made almost entirely on the band saw, and for other projects the band saw figures prominently in the construction. This chapter features two of each.

The projects that can be completed almost solely with the band saw include a shaped letter opener and a band-sawn box that's crafted from a single piece of wood. The projects where the band saw plays a prominent part are an attractive and easy-to-build stationery box and—for those interested in a challenge—a cabriole-leg stool. There's something about the graceful S-curves of these legs that just calls to most woodworkers. Crafting elegant cabriole legs is well within the reach of most woodworkers—so why not answer the call and give it try.

Three of the four projects featured in this chapter are shown here in various stages of construction: a laminated letter opener, a box sawn from a single blank, and a challenging but rewarding cabriole-leg stool.

Letter Opener

Making a letter opener like the one shown in the top left photo is an excellent way to learn how to make compound cuts on the band saw. What's more, this is an excellent project for all those wood scraps you can't quite delegate to the waste bin. You can use almost any wood or woods for this project—use a single solid piece, or try your hand at gluing up some laminated blanks. The more varied the woods, the more interesting the outcome. The two letter openers here were made from a single blank of zebrawood and a blank made by laminating a thin strip of maple between two thicker pieces of mahogany.

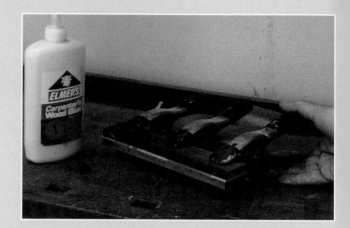

Prepare the blank

To make the letter opener shown here, you'll need a blank that's roughly 1½" wide and 9" long and approximately ⅞" to 1" thick. For more variety, consider gluing up the blank from varying thicknesses and different species of wood, as shown in the top right photo. If you do glue up a blank, make sure to allow it to dry overnight before you start shaping the blank.

EXPLODED VIEW

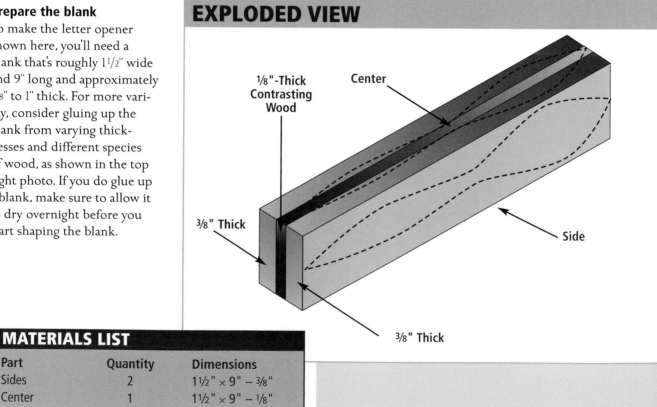

⅛"-Thick Contrasting Wood

Center

⅜" Thick

Side

⅜" Thick

MATERIALS LIST

Part	Quantity	Dimensions
Sides	2	1½" × 9" − ⅜"
Center	1	1½" × 9" − ⅛"

FULL-SIZED PATTERNS

Top   Side

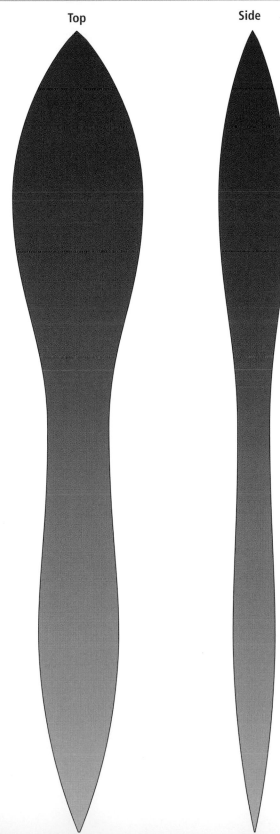

Lay out the patterns

Once your blank is prepared, you can lay out the letter opener patterns onto the blank. Since the letter opener is made using compound cuts, you'll need two patterns, one for the side and one for the top, as illustrated in the drawing at left. We've learned over the years that it's almost always worth the time to make a template for a pattern out of $1/8$" or $1/4$" plywood or hardboard. This saves you the trouble of duplicating or copying a pattern when you go to make a second or third project. Center the template on the blank from side to side and from end to end, and trace around it with a pencil as shown in the top photo. Repeat this for the adjacent side pattern, taking care to align the beginning and end of each pattern.

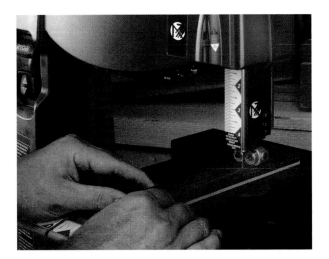

Cut one side

Although you can cut either profile first, many woodworkers prefer to cut the narrower of the two profiles first, as it's often more difficult to cut a workpiece on edge once it's been cut and the waste pieces are taped back on. To make it easier to tape the waste pieces back in place (see the next step), it's best to leave one end of the blank intact. That is, cut the full length of the pattern line, but don't cut through the end of the blank. Instead, back up and cut the other profile line.

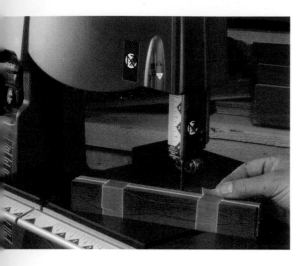

Tape on the waste

Once you've cut one half of the letter opener profile, you'll need to tape the waste back onto the cut blank, as shown in the top photo. This way you can make the second cut. If you didn't tape the pieces back on, not only would you be trying to cut a curved piece on edge (very dangerous), but you'd also lose the pattern that you laid out on the waste piece. After you've taped the waste back in place, take the time to redraw the pattern line on the tape since the tape will obscure the original line.

Cut the other side

With the waste taped back onto the blank, go ahead and cut the second profile of the letter opener, as shown in the middle photo. Make sure to stay on the waste side of the pattern line or you may end up cutting the profile too thin. When done, separate the waste from the curved blank.

Sand the profile

Now you can clean up the rough band-sawn edges of the letter opener and shape it as desired. A drill press fitted with a drum sander as shown in the bottom photo works well for this. You can also shape the edges with a file and sandpaper. You want the cross section of the opener to taper from its center to the edges equally on both sides and to a fine point at the tip. Round over the handle portion for a comfortable grip, and when it's shaped, finish-sand by hand in the direction of the grain and apply your finish of choice.

Band-Sawn Box

Besides being attractive and easy to make, what's truly unique about a band-sawn box is that the band saw is the only power tool you'll need to make it literally from start to finish. A band-sawn box is any box that's made from a single block of wood. Although we've made a simple rectangular box here, the possibilities are endless in terms of shaping. The basic technique described here will work for almost any size blank and shape.

Boxes can have multiple drawers, and they can be stacked vertically or horizontally and even in pyramid form. The only downside to making a band-sawn box out of a single piece of wood is that the blank itself generally needs to be fairly thick. Additionally, you do waste the wood that's cut out from the drawers (more on this later). The dimensions in the materials list are for the box shown here, but virtually any size blank will do (our blank was 3 1/4" wide, 6" long, and 2 1/2" thick).

EXPLODED VIEW

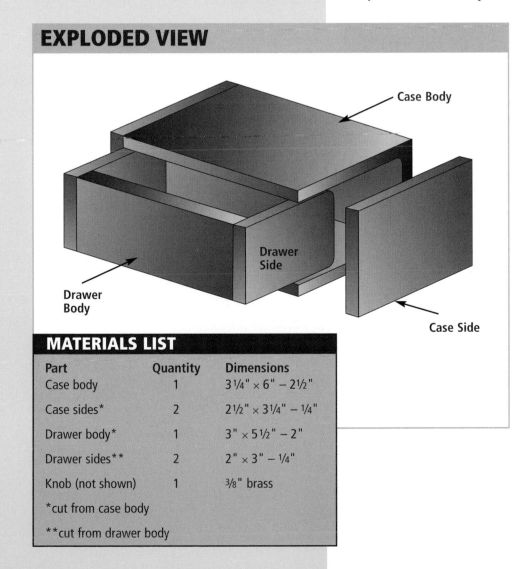

Case Body

Drawer Side

Drawer Body

Case Side

MATERIALS LIST

Part	Quantity	Dimensions
Case body	1	3 1/4" × 6" – 2 1/2"
Case sides*	2	2 1/2" × 3 1/4" – 1/4"
Drawer body*	1	3" × 5 1/2" – 2"
Drawer sides**	2	2" × 3" – 1/4"
Knob (not shown)	1	3/8" brass

*cut from case body

**cut from drawer body

Cut the box sides

To make a band-sawn box, start by cutting off what will end up being the sides of the box. The simplest way to do this is to position the rip fence on your band saw for a 1/4"-wide cut. Then simply push one end and then the other end of the box past the blade, butting the blank against the rip fence as shown in the top photo. Make sure to use a push stick or scrap (as shown) to push the cutoff past the blade as you finish each cut.

Cut out the drawer

Set the sides aside and remove the rip fence. Now you can cut out the recess in the body of the case—the waste piece will become the drawer; see the cutting sequence on page 177 for more on this. Start by placing the case blank on end and then mark cut lines 1/4" in from the edges at the top, bottom, and back of the blank. Raise the upper guide assembly on the saw as needed, turn on the saw, and cut out the waste as shown in the middle photo. As you'll likely be removing a lot of wood—just as if you were resawing (which in fact, you are)—increase the blade tension and take your time with the cut. This is especially important as you near the back corners—you won't be able to make a square corner cut here. Instead, you'll have to make a radiused corner—how tight a radius will depend on your blade width.

Glue the sides onto box

Once you've cut out the drawer, you can glue the sides you cut off earlier back onto the case body. Make sure to replace each side from the end it was cut off by matching up the grain. Then apply a coat of glue to the ends of the case body and clamp the sides in place, taking care that all edges are flush as shown in the bottom photo. Note that the opening for the drawer may tend to close up a bit because of the internal tensions released when you cut out the drawer. If this happens, insert a scrap block and a shim to wedge the opening out as needed to bring its edges flush with the sides.

Slice off the drawer sides

As the glue is drying on the case, you can begin work on the drawer. Start by setting up your rip fence for a $1/4$"-wide cut. Then cut the sides off the drawer as you did on the case body earlier. Here again, you'll want to finish up the cut with a push stick or scrap of wood as shown in the top photo. Set the sides aside for now.

Cut the drawer recess

The next step is to cut out the recess for the drawer. The waste piece here is actually waste—although if it's large enough, you could conceivably get another band-sawn box out of it. As you did with the case body, scribe a

set of $1/4$" cut lines on the drawer blank. But this time you want the lines on the front, back, and bottom of the blank, as illustrated in the drawing below. Stand the blank on end and cut out the waste as shown in the middle photo.

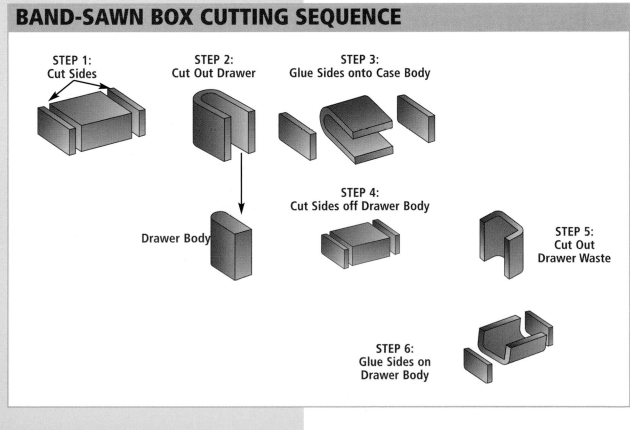

BAND-SAWN BOX CUTTING SEQUENCE

STEP 1: Cut Sides

STEP 2: Cut Out Drawer

STEP 3: Glue Sides onto Case Body

Drawer Body

STEP 4: Cut Sides off Drawer Body

STEP 5: Cut Out Drawer Waste

STEP 6: Glue Sides on Drawer Body

Glue on drawer sides

Once you have the waste cut out of the drawer, you can glue back in place the drawer sides that you cut off previously. Make sure to orient the sides so the grain matches. Apply glue and clamps as shown in the top photo, and allow both the drawer and case to dry overnight before proceeding.

Sand the exteriors

All that's left is to clean up the rough band-sawn surfaces. A stationary belt/disk sander makes quick work of this. Or you can use a portable sander such as a belt or disk sander, but with these it can be difficult to achieve a flat surface. Another way to get a flat surface is to lay a sheet of sandpaper on a known-flat surface (like a workbench or table saw top) and scrub the workpiece back and forth over the sandpaper, as shown in the middle photo. Repeat this for all drawer and case surfaces.

Round over the inside edges

Finally, sand a slight roundover on the inside edges of the case and drawer, as shown in the bottom photo. You may also want to break the sharp edges on the exterior of the case with sandpaper as well. Alternatively, a router fitted with a 1/8" roundover bit will make quick work of this task. When done, apply your finish of choice and install the brass knob.

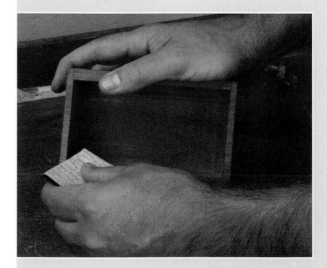

Curved Stationery Box

The gentle curves of the sides and front of the stationery box shown in the top photo add a soft, elegant touch to an otherwise ordinary box. Contrasting wood plugs at the four corners of the top provide visual interest while also helping to make this good-looking box surprisingly easy to make.

The case of the stationery box consists of two curved sides joined to a front and back with tongue-and-groove joints, as illustrated in the exploded view drawing at left. A bottom fits into grooves cut in the front and back. Contrasting plugs fill the grooves near the top of the sides. The top is made up of two sides, a front and back, and a plywood top all joined together with tongue-and-groove joints. The top attaches to the back via a set of brass hinges.

EXPLODED VIEW

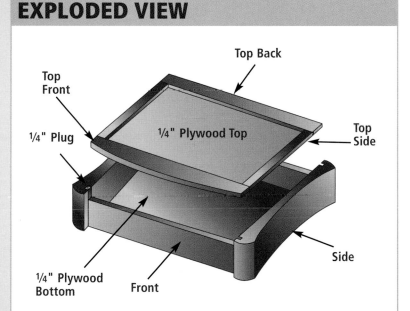

MATERIALS LIST

Part	Quantity	Dimensions
Case sides	2	$2\frac{1}{2}" \times 10" - 1$
Case front/back	2	$2\frac{1}{8}" \times 12" - \frac{3}{8}"$
Case bottom	1	$9" \times 11\frac{1}{2}" - \frac{1}{4}"$ plywood
Top sides	2	$\frac{13}{16}" \times 10\frac{3}{8}" - \frac{3}{8}"$
Top front	1	$1\frac{1}{2}" \times 11\frac{1}{2}" - \frac{3}{8}"$
Top back	1	$\frac{13}{16}" \times 11\frac{1}{2}" - \frac{3}{8}"$
Top	1	$9\frac{1}{2}" \times 10\frac{1}{2}" - \frac{1}{4}"$ plywood
Plugs	4	$\frac{1}{4}" \times \frac{1}{2}" - \frac{1}{4}"$
Hinges	2	$\frac{3}{4}" \times 1" -$ brass

Cut the grooves in the sides

The most reliable way to get a lid or top to fit onto a box properly is to make the box or case first and then build the top to fit the box. Begin work on the stationery box by cutting the case sides to the dimensions in the materials list. Since the sides will be curved later, now is the time to cut any joinery while they're still square. The case sides are joined to the front and back with a simple tongue-and-groove joint; see the detail in the drawing on page 179. Set the rip fence on your table saw to position a groove 1/4" back from the end of each side. Then cut a 1/4" × 3/16" groove as shown in the top photo.

Cut grooves for the bottom

Cut the front and back to size per the materials list. Then cut a 3/16"-deep by 1/4"-wide groove 1/4" up from the bottom edge of the front and back, as shown in the middle photo. Note that we didn't groove the sides for the bottom.

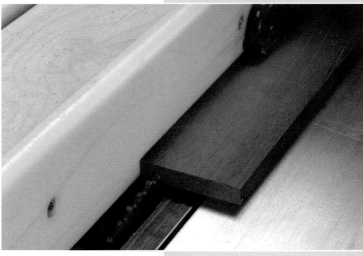

Instead, we glued 1/4" × 1/4" cleats to their bottom edges after the box was assembled to support the sides of the plywood bottom.

Cut tenons on case front and back

The other half of the tongue-and-groove joint—the tongue—can now be cut on the ends of the front and back. The 1/4"-thick tongue is formed by cutting a 1/8"-deep rabbet on the ends, as shown in the bottom photo. Make sure to use a backer board to prevent tearout on the ends of the pieces.

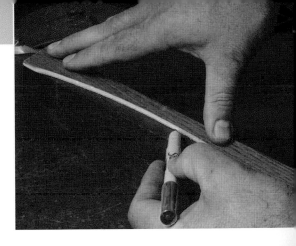

Lay out curves on the sides

With all the joinery complete on the case pieces, you can lay out and cut the curves on the sides. There are three different curves on each side piece: two small curves near the ends, and a large gradual curve from end to end. The small curves start at the inside corner and slope back $1/2$". The long curve begins where the small curves end and is $1/2$" wide at the center. You can make the long curve by bending a flexible stick between the points of the smaller curves; or make a template and trace around this, as shown in the top photo.

Cut the sides to shape

Now you can cut the curve on the sides. Adjust the upper guide assembly as needed and turn on your saw. Feed the side gently into the blade, taking care to stay to the waste side of the marked line, as shown in the middle photo. After you've cut all the curves, sand them smooth. A drum sander mounted in a drill press will quickly smooth the rough band-sawn surfaces. (Note: Save the waste pieces; see below.)

Assemble the case

Before you can assemble the case, you'll need to cut a plywood bottom to size. The most accurate way to do this is to dry-clamp the case parts together. Then measure the opening and add $3/8$" to both dimensions and cut a bottom to this size. To assemble the case, apply glue in the grooves in the sides for the bottom and the grooves in the sides for the front and back. Then place the waste pieces on the curved sides and apply clamps (bottom photo). At this time you can also measure and cut $1/4$" × $1/4$" cleats to fit between the case front and back at the bottom edge of the sides. Attach these with glue and spring clamps to support the bottom at the sides.

Add the plugs

You'll notice that the grooves you cut in the sides extend up past the front and back. Fill these gaps with plugs. You can either cut them from the same wood as the sides to conceal the gap or do what we did and cut them from a contrasting wood to add visual interest to the case. The plugs are 1/4" square and about 1/2" long. We sanded a four-way chamfer on the top of each plug before gluing them in place, as shown in the top photo.

Cut the lid grooves

The case is complete at this point so you can turn your attention to the lid. The lid is made up of a curved front, two sides, and a back. All of these parts are joined together with tongue-and-groove joints. To cut the joints, start by cutting 1/8"-wide by 3/8"-deep grooves centered on the edges of each part—this groove also accepts the tongue cut on the top; see below. We cut the groove on the table saw as shown in the middle photo. A featherboard will help hold the parts in place to keep the groove centered.

Cut the lid tongues

Now you can cut the tongues on the ends of the lid sides to fit into the grooves that you just cut. The tongues are 1/8" thick and 3/8" long. These can be quickly cut on the table saw or band saw, using the rip fence as a stop to define the length of the tongue, as shown in the bottom photo.

Rabbet the top

The top is a piece of $1/4''$ plywood cut to fit in the lid frame. Here again, the most accurate way to do this is to dry-clamp the lid parts together. Then measure the opening and add $5/8''$ to both dimensions and cut a lid to size. Note that we chose a contrasting wood for this for added visual interest. When the top is cut to size, you'll need to cut a rabbet around its perimeter (as shown in the top photo) to create a $1/8''$-thick tongue to fit into the grooves you cut earlier in the lid parts.

Assemble the lid

Now you can assemble the lid. Apply glue to the tongues and grooves as well as the lid tongue—no need to worry about wood movement here, as the top is plywood and gluing it in place will create a strong lid. Apply clamps as shown in the middle photo and allow the lid to dry. Then use a bent stick to lay out the gradual curve on the front, and cut the curve to shape. Sand the band-sawn edges smooth and sand the entire lid and case.

Attach the lid

To complete the stationery box, attach the lid to the back with a set of $3/4'' \times 1''$ brass hinges as shown in the bottom photo. Since these soft and tiny brass screws tend to break easily, make sure to drill pilot holes before driving them in. Also a little dab of wax or paraffin on the screw threads will also help them go in easily without breaking.

Cabriole-Leg Stool

For many woodworkers, a project featuring cabriole legs can often be found on their "someday I'm going to build one of those" lists. What's surprising is that few of these woodworkers have any Queen Anne style furniture in their home. But that doesn't matter. What does matter is that the graceful S-curve of a cabriole leg calls out to them. It says, "If you can make me, you're an accomplished woodworker." And that's all the challenge many of us need to tackle a project like the cabriole-leg stool shown in the top photo.

What may come as a surprise is that it's not that difficult to shape a cabriole leg—the bulk of the shaping is done by making compound cuts on the band saw. The only challenge is smoothing the legs, and this isn't that hard if you follow the step-by-step instructions on pages 188–189. The stool shown here consists of four cabriole legs joined with mortise-and-tenon joints to the front, back, and side rails, as illustrated in the drawing at right. Small shaped blocks called wings serve as transitions between the legs and the rails. A plywood top is covered with batting and fabric to complete the stool.

EXPLODED VIEW

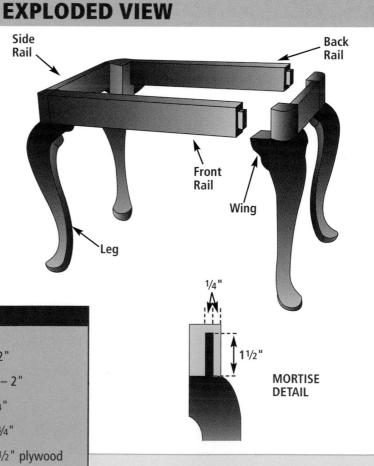

Side Rail

Back Rail

Front Rail

Wing

Leg

MORTISE DETAIL

1/4"

1 1/2"

MATERIALS LIST

Part	Quantity	Dimensions
Legs	4	$2" \times 12\frac{3}{4}" - 2"$
Wings	8	$1\frac{3}{8}" \times 1\frac{11}{16}" - 2"$
Side rails	2	$1\frac{3}{4}" \times 9" - \frac{3}{4}"$
Front/back rails	2	$1\frac{3}{4}" \times 14" - \frac{3}{4}"$
Top	1	$9\frac{1}{4}" \times 14" - \frac{1}{2}"$ plywood

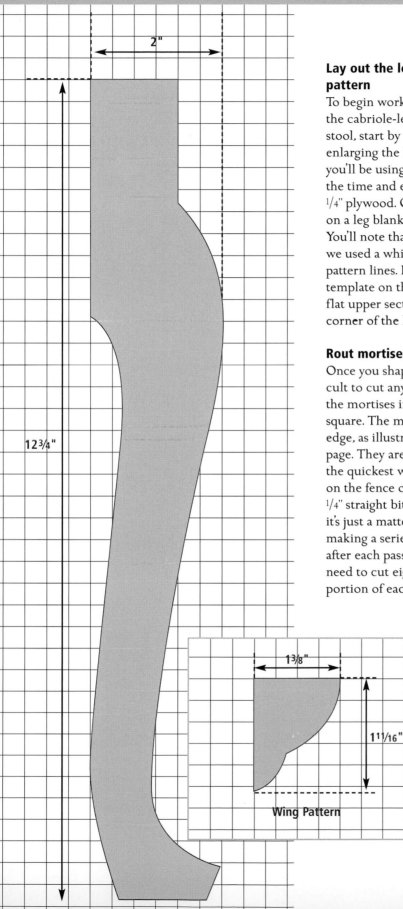

2"

12³⁄₄"

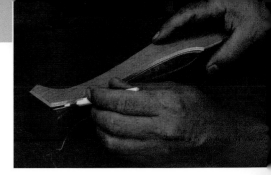

Lay out the leg pattern

To begin work on the cabriole-leg stool, start by enlarging the leg pattern illustrated at left. Since you'll be using the pattern multiple times, it's worth the time and effort to make a template from ¹⁄₈" or ¹⁄₄" plywood. Once you've made the template, place it on a leg blank and trace around it with a pencil. You'll note that because we used walnut for the legs, we used a white pencil so we could easily see the pattern lines. Rotate each blank and trace around the template on the adjacent side, taking care that the flat upper section of the leg patterns connect at one corner of the leg as shown in the top photo.

Rout mortises in the legs

Once you shape a leg on the band saw, it's very difficult to cut any joinery. That's why you should rout the mortises in the legs now while the blank is still square. The mortises are located ¹⁄₄" in from the edge, as illustrated in the drawing on the opposite page. They are ⁵⁄₈" deep and 1¹⁄₂" long. We found that the quickest way to make these was to set up stops on the fence of a table-mounted router fitted with a ¹⁄₄" straight bit, as shown in the bottom photo. Then it's just a matter of lowering the leg onto the bit and making a series of light passes, raising the bit more after each pass until the mortise is fully cut. You'll need to cut eight mortises—two on the back corner portion of each leg.

1³⁄₈"

1¹¹⁄₁₆"

Wing Pattern

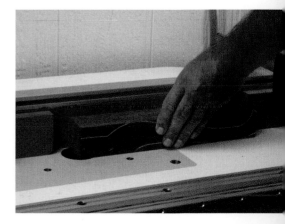

Cut the rail tenons

Before going on to shape the legs, it's a good idea to first cut all the rails to size and then cut the tenons on the ends to fit the mortises you just routed in the legs. These can be quickly cut on the table saw or band saw, using the rip fence as a stop to define the length of the tenon, as shown in the top photo. Make sure to cut a tenon or two on scraps first so that you can sneak up on the perfect fit.

Cut the rail rabbets

Next you can cut a rabbet on the top inside edge of each rail piece. This $3/8'' \times 3/8''$ rabbet accepts the fabric-covered top. Set the rip fence on your table saw or table-mounted router to define the depth of the rabbet (as shown in the middle photo), and then cut the rabbet in each piece with a single pass, or multiple passes as shown here. To complete the rails, round over the ends of the tenons with a four-in-hand rasp or file to match the rounded mortises you routed earlier.

Use stops to define square portion of leg

The top of a cabriole leg is cut square to create a flat area for connecting the rails. Although the front corner of this square portion is rounded (more on this later), the other three corners need to be square. You could make these cuts freehand, but it's a lot more precise to set up your rip fence to define the width of the square portions and place a stop behind the blade to set the length (in our case, 2''). Then it's just a matter of pushing each leg blank into the saw blade until the blank butts up against the stop (as shown in the bottom photo). Now rotate the blank and cut the adjacent side. Repeat this for all four legs.

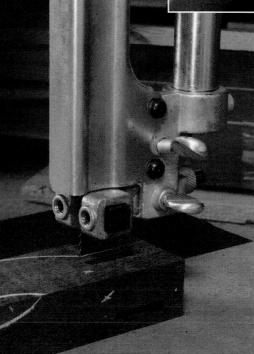

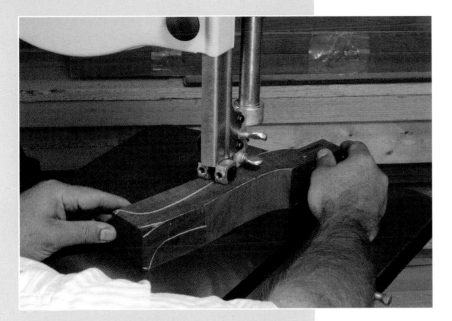

Cut one profile

Now for the fun part—cutting the S-curves. Start by cutting one profile completely as shown in the top photo. Take care to save the waste pieces—you'll be taping them back onto the blank in the next step. Make sure to cut on the waste side of the line. But do try to cut as closely as possible to it—any excess wood you leave here will need to be removed by hand later when you smooth the leg.

Tape the waste back onto leg

Carefully reposition the waste pieces back onto the blank and tape them in place as shown in the middle photo. As there will be numerous waste pieces, you'll need to tape in a couple different locations; you're better off with too much tape than not enough. With the pieces in place, reposition the template on the blank and retrace the pattern lines where they're obscured by the tape, as shown in the inset photo at right.

Cut the second profile

Rotate the blank so the uncut pattern is facing up, and cut the second profile as shown in the bottom photo. We generally make the small cuts first, such as the curve at the foot, before progressing on to the longer cuts. This cutting sequence leaves more wood attached to the blank longer so that it's more stable as you make the final cuts. Repeat this two-part profile-cutting sequence on the remaining three leg blanks.

Cut the wings to shape

With the leg profiles cut, the next step is to cut out the wings that make a smooth transition from the legs to the rails. The wings are simply glued on the flat sections of the legs where the square section stops and the S-curves begin. Each wing has two profiles (like the legs) and therefore requires compound cuts. Cut eight wing blocks to size and then trace the wing pattern on one face of each block—this will be the face of each wing. The second profile comes from the top of the S-curve. To define this, press a block up against a leg so the face of the block is flush at the front edge where the S-curve begins on the leg and trace the profile onto the wing blank. Then cut both profiles on each of the eight wings as shown in the top photo. As these blocks are small, consider using one of the techniques described on page 59 for cutting small pieces safely.

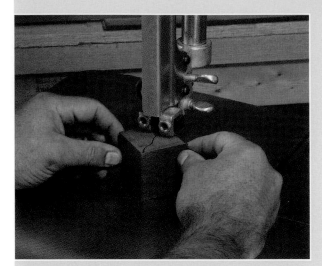

Glue the wings onto the legs

Now you can glue a pair of wings onto each leg as shown in the middle photo. Since there are no flat clamping surfaces here, you'll need to use your hands as clamps. Apply a generous coat of glue to the flat face of the wing and press it in place on the leg, taking care to align the surfaces. Hold the wing fixed in place for 2 minutes and then move on to the next wing. Repeat for the remaining legs and allow the glue to dry overnight before proceeding with the shaping.

Mark reference lines on the legs

At this point you have four legs that resemble cabriole legs. The S-curve is there, but it's rough and the edges or corners are sharp. The first thing to do is to smooth the band-sawn surfaces. If you want to do this by hand, use a spokeshave. Alternatively (and the purists would cringe), you can smooth the surfaces using a drum sander fitted in a drill press or portable drill. Whichever method you choose, smooth all four faces of each leg. Then to round over the corners of the curves, use a pencil to strike 1/4" reference marks on each face of the legs, as shown in the bottom photo. To do this, use your fingers as a depth gauge and run the pencil along the face of each curve.

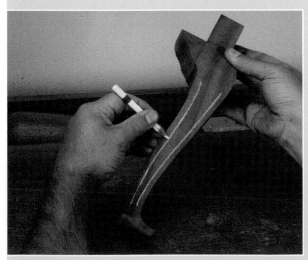

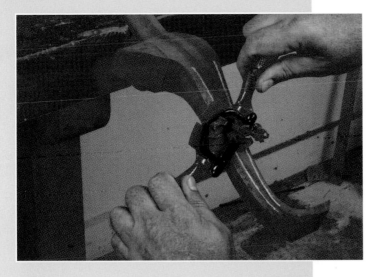

Use a spokeshave to shape the legs

Now you can begin to round over the sharp corners of the legs. Clamp the square portion of a leg in the bench vise as shown in the top photo. Then use a spokeshave to cut a flat between two adjacent marked lines—you're effectively chamfering the corners. When you've completed a flat, angle the spokeshave to one side and knock the corner that you just created with the chamfer; repeat for the other side of the original flat. Continue angling the spokeshave and shaving until you've turned the original flat into a rounded edge. Repeat this for each corner of each of the four legs. When you're done, sand each leg smooth.

Assemble the stool

With the legs shaped and sanded and the rails already complete, you can assemble the stool. Take the time to dry-clamp the parts together first so that you can fine-tune a joint or wing as needed to make the parts snug up nice and flat. When you're satisfied with the fit, apply glue to the mortise-and-tenon joints and clamp the legs to the rails as shown in the middle photo. Allow the glue to dry overnight.

Add the top

To complete the cabriole stool, add the top as shown in the bottom photo. You'll note that before the top will fit into the rabbets in the rails, you'll first need to remove some waste at the top of each leg to form a corner, as shown in the inset photo below. The top is made by cutting a piece of $1/2$" plywood roughly $1/4$" to $3/8$" smaller than the opening in the top. This allows room for batting and fabric. Advanced upholstery skills are not necessary here, as you can simply staple the batting/fabric to the underside of the top. Your local upholstery shop can also make a nice cushion for you—just bring in the finished stool and they'll make one to fit.

INDEX

METRIC EQUIVALENCY CHART

Inches to millimeters and centimeters

inches	mm	cm	inches	cm	inches	cm
1/8	3	0.3	9	22.9	30	76.2
1/4	6	0.6	10	25.4	31	78.7
3/8	10	1.0	11	27.9	32	81.3
1/2	13	1.3	12	30.5	33	83.8
5/8	16	1.6	13	33.0	34	86.4
3/4	19	1.9	14	35.6	35	88.9
7/8	22	2.2	15	38.1	36	91.4
1	25	2.5	16	40.6	37	94.0
1 1/4	32	3.2	17	43.2	38	96.5
1 1/2	38	3.8	18	45.7	39	99.1
1 3/4	44	4.4	19	48.3	40	101.6
2	51	5.1	20	50.8	41	104.1
2 1/2	64	6.4	21	53.3	42	106.7
3	76	7.6	22	55.9	43	109.2
3 1/2	89	8.9	23	58.4	44	111.8
4	102	10.2	24	61.0	45	114.3
4 1/2	114	11.4	25	63.5	46	116.8
5	127	12.7	26	66.0	47	119.4
6	152	15.2	27	68.6	48	121.9
7	178	17.8	28	71.1	49	124.5
8	203	20.3	29	73.7	50	127.0

mm = millimeters   cm = centimeters

Band Saw Fundamentals photo credits

Photo courtesy of Bridgewood (www.bridgewood.com): page 14 (bottom right photo).

Photos courtesy of Carter Products (www.carterproducts.com): page 31 (top photo), page 160 (top right photo).

Photos courtesy of Delta Machinery (www.deltamachinery.com): page 9 (top photo), page 22.

Photos courtesy of Jet Tools (www.jettools.com): page 9 (bottom two photos), page 10, page 15 (bottom photo), page 33 (top photo).

Photos courtesy of Kreg Tool Company (www.kregtool.com): page 33 (middle photo), page 34 (top and middle photos).

Photos courtesy of Laguna Tools (www.lagunatools.com): page 1, page 23.

Photo courtesy of Lenox (www.lenoxsaw.com): page 26.

Photo courtesy of Makita U.S.A., Inc (www.makita.com): page 21 (top photo).

Photo courtesy of Milwaukee Electric Tool (www.milwaukeetool.com): page 11 (top photo).

Photos courtesy of Ryobi (www.ryobitools.com): page 8, page 21 (bottom photo), page 32 (middle photo).

Photo courtesy of Woodhaven (www.woodhaven.com): page 35 (top left photo).